866

WAFFEN-SS

HITLER'S BLACK GUARD
AT WAR

WAFFEN-SS

HITLER'S BLACK GUARD AT WAR

CHRISTOPHER AILSBY

BARNES
&NOBLE
BOOKS
NEW YORK

This edition published by Barnes & Noble, Inc.,
by arrangement with Brown Packaging Books Ltd.
1997 Barnes & Noble Books

M 10 9 8 7 6 5 4 3 2 1

ISBN: 0 7607 0716 2

Conceived and produced by
Brown Packaging Books Ltd.
Bradley's Close
74/77 White Lion Street
London N1 9PF

Editor: Peter Darman
Design: Wilson Design Associates

Printed in Singapore by Star Standard

Photographic credits
Christopher Ailsby Historical Archives: 2-3, 6-7, 9, 20, 21, 24,
25, 27, 35, 36, 46-47, 50, 51, 52-53, 54, 66, 66-67, 69, 70, 71, 73,
74, 80, 82, 83, 86, 90, 101, 102, 138, 139, 140, 141, 142-43,
144-45, 146, 149, 150-51, 152, 154-55, 156, 168, 169
Camera Press: 166-67, 172, 172-73
Peter Newark's Military Pictures: 38, 81, 112 (all four), 136, 155
TRH Pictures: 8, 10-11, 12, 13, 14, 15, 16-17, 28-29, 30-31, 32, 33,
37, 41, 52, 56, 58-59, 59, 60 (both), 61, 62, 63, 64, 64-65, 76, 77,
78-79, 88-89, 91, 92-93, 93, 94 (both), 96-97, 97, 98-99, 104,
105 (both), 106, 107, 110-11, 114, 114-15, 116, 118, 118-19, 126-27,
133, 134-35, 157, 161, 162-63, 163, 164-65, 174-75
TRH Pictures via Espadon: 18-19, 22-23, 26, 39, 42-43, 44, 45, 48,
49, 55, 68-69, 85, 87, 95, 100, 120-21, 123, 124, 125, 146-47, 148, 159,
170-71, back cover

Artwork credits
Aerospace Publishing Ltd.: 40, 84, 153, 158, 160
Orbis Publishing Ltd.: 34, 57, 109, 129, 130, 131, 132, 133, 136

To Suzanne Norville and Edward Holland, for all their help and
encouragement during the writing of this book

CONTENTS

CHAPTER 1

RACIAL WARRIORS

Indoctrinated to believe in the superiority of themselves and their National Socialist cause, the soldiers of the SS were the Third Reich's elite. Strict racial and physical standards were set for entry, and the training of SS soldiers stressed aggression and placed an emphasis on small-unit tactics. Under such progressive leaders as Felix Steiner and Paul Hausser, the armed SS became an excellent fighting machine.

Left: Waffen-SS soldiers on the Eastern Front. For the ideologically indoctrinated soldiers of the Waffen-SS, the war in Russia was a holy crusade against Bolshevism and 'subhumanity'.

In the early days of Nazism, Adolf Hitler was surrounded by the unwieldy Sturmabteilung (SA) – Brownshirts – tough, unemployed ex-soldiers who were recruited by Ernst Röhm to protect Nazi speakers at public meetings.

The Brownshirts contained many undesirable elements, and Hitler realised the necessity of organising a more dedicated elite personal guard: men of proven calibre, of Nordic blood and of good character. They had to act as bodyguard and spearhead with an unequivocal allegiance to Hitler. They had to protect him and important members of his party. In March 1923 they consisted of just two men – Josef Berchtold and Julius Schreck – who called themselves the 'Stabswache' (Staff Guard). Two months later a new unit, the Stosstrupp *Adolf Hitler*, commanded by Josef Berchtold, was formed. In August 1923, a certain Heinrich Himmler joined

Hitler's Nazional Sozialistische Deutsche Arbeiter Partei (the NSDAP), the National Socialist German Workers' Party. Hitler's 9 November 1923 Munich Putsch, his attempt to spark a national revolution, ended in fiasco. Hitler was incarcerated in Landsberg prison and the NSDAP was banned. Himmler returned to Landshut where he acted as general secretary to Gregor Strasser, who, in September 1926, was appointed Reich propaganda leader of the NSDAP. Himmler accompanied him to party headquarters as his secretary. In April 1925, Hitler, now released, ordered his chauffeur and personal bodyguard, Julius Schreck, to raise this new shock troop. A few weeks later it was named the Schutz Staffel (Protection Squad). The new SS was to be organised on a national basis; each major city was called upon to provide one leader and 10 of its best men, but by 1928 it had only

Above: The abortive 1923 Munich putsch. Troops loyal to Adolf Hitler in Munich on 9 November. The fiasco did give the Nazi Party a sacred relic: the so-called Blood Banner. When the Nazis were fired on during the putsch, the flag was splattered with blood. It was subsequently used to consecrate the banners of SS units.

280 members. Himmler's organising ability had not gone unnoticed, and to rectify this situation he was appointed Deputy SS Leader and then National Leader in January 1929, with the rank of SS-Oberführer. At this point he commanded approximately 1000 men and the organisation was still a part of Röhm's SA. To strengthen his own position, Himmler began gradually to assert the separation of the SS from the SA, and brought in biological criteria and the concept of racial purity into new recruitment plans, as a way to trawl through the large number of applications from ex-

Freikorps (right-wing ex-soldiers) and unemployed bourgeois volunteers. The army, which perceived Röhm and the SA as rivals, took a favourable view of the SS as a force. This encouragement, together with Himmler's organisational skills concentrating on the SS's breadth of function and growth in size, rapidly provided him with a personal power base. By 1930, the SS numbered 2727 men; in June 1932, when the SA was officially banned, the SS had grown to 30,000 – approximately 10 per cent of the SA's strength. On 30 January 1933, Hitler became Reich Chancellor, by which time the SS had secretly recruited 52,000 more members.

A decree of 26 April 1933 established the Geheime Staats Polizeiamt (Gestapa), which was later to be renamed Geheime Staats Polizei (Gestapo), as a new department of the Prussian state police. The Gestapo became the target for Himmler. By this time the SS had been divided into two distinct groups: the Allgemeine-SS, which fulfilled a police function and was basically part time, and the newly emergent Bewaffnete-SS (Armed SS), which was military in appearance and full-time.

Himmler's hunger for power continued. He became Munich's chief of police after Hitler became Chancellor in January 1933. This modest post enabled him gradually to gain control of the entire German police network except in Prussia, where Hermann Göring was Minister of the Interior. But he finally achieved complete control in 1936. Through Reinhard Heydrich, his second-in-command, and the Party's own security organisation, the Sicherheitsdienst, or SD, he formed an intelligence service that covered internal and external operations.

After Hitler came to power in January 1933, he decided that he was in need of a Praetorian Guard. The state-provided protection rendered by the Reichswehr (army) or police elements could not in his eyes be entirely replied upon. He therefore decreed that there be formed a new, full-time, armed SS unit, whose primary role would be exclusively to escort him wherever he was in Germany. 'Sepp' Dietrich, one of Hitler's closest associates, was entrusted with the formation of the unit.

Dietrich undertook the task with zeal and by 17 March 1933 the embryo of a new Headquarters Guard, named the SS-Stabswache

Below: Members of the original Stosstrupp Adolf Hitler. *This was formed as a bodyguard for the leader of the Nazi Party, Adolf Hitler. It was the forerunner of the Schutz Staffel (Protection Squad) – the SS. Unlike the Brownshirts, the SS was never conceived of as a mass movement; rather, as a small, dedicated elite.*

Berlin, was founded. It comprised 120 hand-picked volunteers, of whom some were former members of the original Stosstrupp *Adolf Hitler* and whose loyalty to the Führer was unswerving. Two months later, the unit was reformed as the SS Sonderkommando *Zossen* and enlarged with three training companies. The terms of engagement for the unit were expanded and the unit could now be employed for armed police and anti-terrorist activities, as well as the guard duties it already undertook. There was another metamorphosis during the next months, when a further three companies were formed as the SS Sonderkommando *Jüterbog*.

The oath to Hitler

A rally, the first since 1929 at Nuremberg, was held on 31 August to 3 September 1933. It was known as the Parteitag des Siegers, or Victor's Party Rally, and marked the Nazi accession to power on 30 January 1933. At this rally Hitler formally recognised the *Adolf Hitler SS* Standart (regiment) and the dedication of the SS Standarten took place. This was formed from SS-Sonderkommando *Zossen* and SS-Sonderkommando *Jüterbog*. Dietrich received the banner with the name 'Adolf Hitler' on the box that surmounted it. The two sonderkommandos were granted the honour and right to wear the name 'Adolf Hitler' on a cuff band on the left arm. The merged formation was renamed the *Leibstandarte SS Adolf Hitler*. The members of the *Leibstandarte* took a personal oath of

Right: A Nazi Party rally at Nuremberg, with SA men in the foreground. By early 1934, by which time Hitler had become Chancellor, the SA had outlived its usefulness. The result was the 'Night of the Long Knives', when Ernst Röhm, the leader of the SA, and his commanders were executed, the SS providing firing squads.

allegiance to Hitler. This dispelled any thoughts that they were anything but his personal cohort. Himmler theoretically had control over the unit, but in reality the ultimate director of its function was Hitler himself. In addition, his friendship with 'Sepp' Dietrich meant the *Leibstandarte* exercised an independence within the SS that no other unit enjoyed.

By late 1933, the *Leibstandarte* was garrisoned in Berlin. Its duties were further expanded and encompassed all walks of Hitler's life. Its members served as adjutants, waiters, general servants and drivers. Their ceremonial duties included forming the Reich Chancellery guard and other state and party functions, where they held the place of honour at the end of the parade.

The Leibstandarte was used in the Röhm Putsch, the 'Night of the Long Knives' in July 1934, when the power of the SA was destroyed with the killing of Röhm and its other leaders. It was instrumental in the arrests and many of the killings. The number of executions that took place by the *Leibstandarte* firing squads is not known, but it is reported that there were in the order of 40 executioners employed. The *Leibstandarte*'s 'first blooding' was over when the shooting finally ended on 2 July. As a reward for its loyalty and involvement, Dietrich was promised by Hitler that he would see that the *Leibstandarte* would become a fully equipped regiment. To this end, a rare honour was to be conferred on it in early October 1934 when it was decided that it should be fully motorised. At this time the Reichswehr was in the main still horse-drawn, and this decision led to whispers of discontent in military circles. The Political Readiness Detachments were to be reorganised into battalions and then amalgamated within the *Leibstandarte*

Above: The Hitler Youth on parade. The male youth of Nazi Germany proved a rich recruiting ground for the Waffen-SS. Fit, eager and imbued with the tenets of National Socialism, they made excellent soldiers. Hitler was to state that the 'youngsters who come from the Hitler Youth are fanatical fighters.'

under Himmler's orders of 14 December 1934.

How were the recruits selected and indoctrinated in the SS-Totenkopfverbände (Death's Head units – concentration camp guards) and the SS-Verfügungstruppe (SS military units)? Young university educated men, products of the national Youth Movement, were encouraged to join the SS. Many joined whose motivation was purely power and a fear of a return to the chaos and instability of the Depression years. Predominately lawyers and economists, these men tended to gravitate to the SD or the

SS-Hauptampt (SS-Main Office). Some volunteered for the fledgling SS-Verfügungstruppe, although a greater proportion of the SS-Verfügungstruppe's officer cadres were middle-class soldiers who transferred from the Reichswehr. The officer classes, on the other hand, were initially more difficult to persuade. Men from this background were not going to be impressed by the undisciplined rabble which comprised 90 per cent of SS membership in the early days. To rectify the situation, Himmler implemented cleansing programmes that led to 60,000 men being expelled from the SS between 1933 and 1935 in an attempt to rid it of outright criminals, homosexuals, alcoholics, the 'professionally unemployed' and anyone who could not prove he had no Jewish blood. Standards were tightened for admission: racial purity, physical fitness, height and the lack of a criminal record became prerequisites for acceptance. For a period the *Leibstandarte* would not even consider a man for admission into its ranks if he had a single tooth filled. The result of these two policies was that by 1938 12 per cent of SS officers holding the rank of Standartenführer or higher came from the military aristocracy.

At the other end of the scale, at the age of 18 a Hitlerjugend – Hitler Youth – could become an SS-Bewerber, or applicant. After a short probationary period he took the oath of allegiance to Adolf Hitler. At the age of 19 he went into the Labour Service and then into the armed forces. He returned to the SS,

Right: Theodor Eicke, commander of the SS-Totenkopfverbände and later the Totenkopf Division. *It was Eicke who shot Ernst Röhm in his cell during the 'Night of the Long Knives'. He instilled into his men a fanatical hatred of the enemies of National Socialism, which often resulted in them committing atrocities.*

still as a candidate, if he elected not to remain in the armed forces as a regular or non-commissioned officer candidate after his two years' service. The candidate was given special ideological training, the principles of the SS being thoroughly explained, in particular the marriage order and code of honour of the SS. Subject to fulfilling all the special requirements, the SS candidate was finally accepted as an SS man.

Entry standards

Pre-war there were different qualification standards for the SS-Totenkopfverbände recruits and those of the SS-Verfügungstruppe. To qualify to join the *Leibstandarte* or SS-Verfügungstruppe, a recruit had to be at least 1.80m (5ft 11in) and later 1.84m (6ft 0.5in) tall and between the ages of 17 and 22. To join the SS-Totenkopfverbände the height restriction was only 1.71m (5ft 7.5in), which was later reduced to 1.69m (5ft 6.7in), and the upper age limit was 26. Neither organisation insisted on educational qualifications, and so before 1938, 40 per cent of SS recruits had only received what could be termed primary school education. Insistence on being able to prove Aryan descent, being in good physical and mental

condition and to have clean police records were more important.

The SS had good material to work with, for despite the fact that nearly half the recruits had received only minimal education, their stature and fitness were of an extremely high standard. Himmler boasted in 1937 that 'we still choose only 15 out of every 100 candidates who present themselves.'

Service in the SS-Totenkopfverbände for non-commissioned officers and men was 12 years. Since this duty did not count as military service, Hitler ordered that volunteers be chosen from among those 'who, as a rule, have served their compulsory military duty in the army'. Most of the men recruited for the SS-Totenkopfverbände before the issuance of the Führer decree were youngsters between 17 and 19, and this practice did not altogether cease after 1938.

Among Himmler's initial criteria for entry into the SS were anti-Christian beliefs. Theodor Eicke, the commander of the SS-Totenkopfverbände, for example, aimed to create among his men a hatred for the churches as enemies of National Socialism. He initiated a vehement anti-religious campaign, and many individuals who clung to

Above: SS-Oberstgruppenführer Paul Hausser, appointed to be the inspector of the military units of the SS before the war. Under his expert guidance the Waffen-SS became a highly efficient military unit. Hausser went on the become one of the finest Waffen-SS commanders of World War II, being known as 'Papa' to his men.

their beliefs were victimised mercilessly. Eicke held the view that the SS-Totenkopfverbände constituted an elite within the elite structure of the SS. This elitism grew from his concept that the most dangerous political enemies of the state were incarcerated in the concentration camps, and that Hitler had given sole responsibility for guarding and running the camps to the SS-Totenkopfverbände. To reinforce his principles Eicke reiterated them habitually in orders, circulars, and memoranda. The whole of the SS-Totenkopfverbände training he based on elitism, toughness and comradeship. A regime of ruthless discipline was placed upon the organisation, and the slightest infractions of SS rules brought harsh and often brutal punishment.

Each month was organised into three weeks in training, followed by one week of guard duty within the concentration camp. Participation in camp guard duty was meant to give individuals exposure to the prisoners and conditions in the camps. This experience Eicke felt would confirm the lessons learned by the SS man during his training. His belief would strengthen that the prisoners were inferior but implacable enemies of the Reich, against which the SS had to wage an unending struggle. The behaviour of the SS-Totenkopfverbände suggests he created an atmosphere conducive to indoctrinated fanaticism, which gave rise to the excesses they perpetrated, both on and off the battlefield.

Political indoctrination

The political indoctrination of the SS men was divided into three broad areas. The first dealt with the history of the Nazi Party, and included an examination of the party programme. The second involved the history and racial beliefs of the SS, with special emphasis placed upon the SS-Totenkopfverbände. The third and most important part required a careful analysis of the enemies of National Socialism. In order of importance these were: the Jews, Freemasons, Bolsheviks, and the churches.

On becoming the new inspector of concentration camps and prisons in 1934, Eicke reorganised and enlarged the SS-Totenkopfverbände into five numbered sturmbanne, or battalions: I *Oberbayern*, II *Elbe*, III *Sachsen*, IV *Ostfriesland* and V *Thüringen*. In 1937 the five battalions were again reorganised, this time into three standarten which carried the designations *Oberbayern*, *Brandenburg*, and *Thüringen*. They were stationed in Dachau, Oranienburg and Frankenberg respectively. A few months later, Standarte *Thüringen* was transferred from Frankenberg to the Buchenwald concentration camp in Weimar. After the Austrian *Ans-*

chluss in March 1938, a fourth regiment bearing the name *Ostmark* was established at Linz, later providing the guards for Mauthausen camp. As of 1 April 1938 the organisation of the SS-Totenkopfverbände was fixed at four standarten of three sturmbanne with three infantry companies comprising 148 men each, one machine-gun company comprising 150 men, and medical, transport and communications units. Hitler formed a division from the Totenkopf units during the winter of 1939.

On 16 March 1935, Hitler officially established the SS-Verfügungstruppe, although at the time it already consisted of 11 battalions (on the same day he reintroduced military conscription, in direct contravention of the Treaty of Versailles). The intention was always that the SS-Verfügungstruppe would benefit from the highest possible standards of training available. To facilitate this, two highly regarded former army officers, Paul Hausser and Felix Steiner, were recruited. Both were ultimately to become among the finest field commanders in the Waffen-SS.

A special inspectorate of the SS-Verfügungstruppe was created on 1 October 1936 to supervise administration and military training. The new inspectorate had the objective of moulding the mainly ill-trained and far-flung units of the SS-Verfügungstruppe into an efficient fighting force. SS-Oberstgruppenführer und Generaloberst der Waffen-SS Paul Hausser, who was to become known affectionately as 'Papa' Hausser to his men, was chosen to be inspector of the SS-Verfügungstruppe, though he had only just been appointed inspector of the SS-Junkerschule (Officer Schools) at Bad Tölz and Brunswick. The inspectorate fused the SS-Verfügungstruppe into a formidable organisation and supervised its administration and training. Hausser remained inspector until the outbreak of the World War II, when he took command of what was to become the *Das Reich* division of the Waffen-SS.

Felix Steiner, on the other hand, was the luminary when it came to the actual training programme of the SS-Verfügungstruppe. Steiner believed strongly in the creation of elite, highly mobile groups whose training put the emphasis on team

Below: SS officer cadets at the Bad Tölz SS Officer School. More than anything else, it was the officer schools which turned out soldiers who epitomised the spirit of the Waffen-SS: men who displayed blind obedience to Hitler and his orders, who were loyal and tough and led by example, often at the expense of their own lives.

Above: A pre-war photograph of the Leibstandarte SS Adolf Hitler, *which later became one of the finest fighting units on any side in World War II. Its members were the physical manifestation of what the novelist Ernst Jünger wrote in 1919: 'a new man, the storm soldier, the elite of central Europe. A completely new race.'*

work rather than mindless obedience. His ideas had been formulated and refined during World War I, when he served as a junior infantry officer, and later as commander of a machine-gun company, witnessing the formation of 'battle groups', which had greatly impressed him.

As their value became recognised, Steiner's reforms gradually filtered throughout the SS-Verfügungstruppe hierarchy. In concert with his 'battle group' ideology he promoted a strict physical programme. He structured a recruit's day, which began with a rigorous hour's PT at 0600 hours, with a pause afterwards for breakfast of porridge and mineral water. This was followed by intensive weapons training, target practice and unarmed combat sessions. The day was broken by a hearty lunch, then resumed with a comparatively short but intensive drill session. The afternoon was

then punctuated by a stint of scrubbing, cleaning, scouring and polishing, and rounded off with a run or a couple of hours on the sports field. As a result of his men spending more time on the athletics fields and in cross-country running than on the parade ground, they developed standards of fitness and endurance which enabled them to perform such feats as covering 3km (1.8 miles) in full kit in 20 minutes. The training programme was interrupted three times a week by ideological lectures.

Those who successfully completed the course took the SS oath,

which took place in Hitler's presence. The oath was a major ingredient in the SS mystique, binding each successful candidate in unswerving loyalty to Adolf Hitler.

The candidate now had to spend a year in one of the SS infantry or cavalry schools, before returning to Munich to swear another oath binding himself to obey Himmler's marriage laws. This was an attempt to replace the Christian rites of marriage, christening and death. Marriages no longer took place in churches but in the open under a lime tree, or in an SS building decorated with life runes, fir twigs and sunflowers. The proof of Aryan ancestry was designed to protect racial and physical purity.

To be eligible for a commission in the SS-Verfügungstruppe, officer cadets had to have served for a minimum of two years in the ranks, which initially meant in the Reichswehr. Officers enlisted for 25 years, NCOs for 12 and privates for four, with basic training being the same for all groups.

The SS brotherhood

An innovation introduced by Eicke and emulated by Steiner was designed to break down the rigid divisions between ranks, which had always existed in the army. Officers and NCOs were encouraged to talk and mix with their men to get to know them as individuals. They competed in teams against each other on the sports field. Off-duty they addressed each other as *kamerad* rather than by rank.

On 17 August 1938, Hitler defined the raison d'être of the SS-Verfügungstruppe as being an armed force at his personal disposal, stating that it was not a part of the armed or police forces already in existence. Therefore it was able to be legitimately trained by the Reichsführer-SS in Nazi theories of race and also to be manned by volunteers who had completed their duty in the Reichsarbeitsdienst, the Reich Labour Service. The Führer decree also stated that in time of war, elements of the Totenkopfverbände would reinforce the SS-Verfügungstruppe. If mobilised, it was to be used firstly by the commander-in-chief of the army under army jurisdiction, making it subject to military law and order, but still remaining a branch of the NSDAP and owing its allegiance ultimately to that organisation. In the event of an emergency within Germany, the SS-Verfügungstruppe would be under Hitler's control via Himmler.

The remarkable growth of the Waffen-SS must be attributed to Gottlob Berger rather than Himmler. He was generally able to outmanoeuvre and outwit his military counterparts with a cunning cocktail of diplomacy, threat and duplicity. His successes also encouraged him to undertake increasingly ambitious schemes to expand the wartime rôle of the SS, thus fulfilling the desires of his Reichsführer. Berger was appointed by Himmler to command the SS-Hauptampt, with responsibility, among other duties, for recruitment. One of the functions of the district leaders of the Allgemeine-SS had always been recruiting for the SS, but with the threat of impending war it became necessary to centralise and consolidate this increasingly important rôle. The establishment of a nationwide SS recruiting network was Berger's first task.

The search for manpower

On 1 December 1939 Berger created the Ergänzungsamt der Waffen-SS within the SS-Hauptamt, with himself as its chief. Her immediately spotted that three previously untapped sources of manpower were available to SS-Verfügungstruppe recruitment: the SS-Totenkopfverbände, the wartime reserves of the same organisation, and a large proportion of the ordinary police (Hitler had already agreed to the formation of a third SS-Verfügungstruppe Standarte, *Der Führer*, mainly composed of Austrians and based in Vienna and Klagenfurt).

By the summer of 1939 the armed units of the SS were ready and eager to test themselves on the battlefield. Highly trained and motivated, all ranks believed they would repay the faith placed in them by Hitler and Himmler. They eagerly awaited their baptism of fire, determined to destroy Nazi Germany's enemies.

CHAPTER 2

BAPTISM OF FIRE

The contribution of the armed SS in the 1939 Polish Campaign was negligible, but the Blitzkrieg did witness for the first time the qualities of dash and bravery that were peculiar to SS soldiers. German Army commanders were unimpressed, but the Führer took a different view, which resulted in rapid expansion of Himmler's legions after the Polish campaign had finished.

Left: Soldiers of the Leibstandarte *fighting Polish troops on the outskirts of Pabianice during the war in Poland in September 1939. The* Leibstandarte *was attached to the 10th Army.*

The German plan for the invasion of Poland, codenamed Fall Weiss or Case White, involved two Army Groups comprising five armies, totalling some one and a half million soldiers. The political situation, as viewed by the Nazi leaders, demanded the opening of the war with powerful surprise attacks, which would lead to rapid results, and this was only possible if armoured units were used. Army Group South, consisting of the 7th, 10th and 14th Armies under General von Rundstedt, and Army Group North, consisting of the 3rd and 4th Armies under General Fedor von Bock, were formed to carry out the operation. The main push was to involve 3rd Army and 10th Army, which together would form the arms of a massive pincer movement, the target – the Polish capital Warsaw. The 3rd Army would form the upper arm of the pincer, driving down from its launch point in East Prussia, while 10th Army would drive eastwards then turn north to approach Warsaw from the southwest of the city. Panzer Division *Kempf* was part of 3rd Army in the north and would launch its attack from Niedenburg in East Prussia, with its initial target the tough Polish defensive position at Mlava, northwest of Warsaw.

In view of the heavy French superiority in the west, the attack on Poland had to be handled rapidly and decisively so that the weak German forces on the western front could be reinforced as soon as Poland seemed defeated. If the French army with its 99 divisions and 25,000 armoured combat vehicles, reinforced in mid-September by two British divisions, had attacked before victory was secured in Poland, Germany might have lost the war at the outset.

On 28 August at 2230 at the Chancellery in Berlin, Sir Neville Henderson, the British ambassador, met Hitler to deliver another letter from the British Government. Henderson's observation was that 'Hitler was once again friendly and reasonable and appeared to be not dissatisfied with the answer which I had brought him. Our conversation lasted for well over an hour.' Hitler

Below: Motorcycles of the Leibstandarte's *reconnaissance section. By September 1939, Hitler's bodyguard was a fully motorised unit, making it ideal for fulfilling a reconnaissance and flank-protection role. In Poland it was used for such duties, being rushed from one sector of the front to another.*

Right: German horse-drawn supplies move in Poland on their way towards the front. Contrary to popular opinion, the vast majority of German Army units at the beginning of World War II were not motorised. This is why the motorised units of the SS were so valuable to army commanders during the Blitzkrieg.

cunningly concealed the fact that he had SS-Obergruppenführer Heydrich poised to undertake the deception that would afford him the excuse for the invasion of Poland.

On 29 August at 1915 hours Henderson again went to the Chancellery, this time to receive Hitler's reply to the British government's letter. It was starkly uncompromising. Hitler summed up the situation by stating that the Polish problem must be settled peacefully on German terms by the following day or he would use force. The die was cast.

Grand deception

On 30 August the Polish mobilisation was officially announced. Hitler could wait no longer and on the next day he gave the order to invade Poland at 0445 hours. The time had come to undertake the deception he perceived necessary to legitimise the invasion. SS-Sturmbannführer Alfred Naujocks was chosen by Heydrich to lead the simulated attack on the Gleiwitz radio stations. Naujocks became an official of the Amt VI of the SS security service and was one of the most audacious commanders of the SD. At 1600 hours on 31 August Heydrich alerted Naujocks in Gleiwitz and ordered him to be at the radio station at 1945 hours that evening.

Corpses from the Dachau concentration camp were expected to arrive at approximately 2125 hours, loaded on lorries. The dead 'Polish soldiers' could then be scattered 'convincingly' around the radio station. The deception party arrived on time at the station, finding a 1.8m

(6ft) high wire fence surrounding it, but the two attached buildings which were used for living quarters were unguarded. The German operational staff of the station were not privy to Heydrich's plan.

On reaching the broadcasting studios, Naujocks and his men began making as much noise as possible, hoping to give the impression that the station was under attack by a large Polish insurgent force. The ceiling of the studio received several shots, adding to the bedlam and petrifying the radio personnel. The staff of the station, who had by this time decided that resistance to the strangers was futile, surrendered, and were handcuffed and taken to the basement. Meanwhile a flaw was discovered in the plan: Naujocks and his men did not know how to operate the radio equipment. The SS men were frantically turning dials and flipping switches until they finally found the storm switch. This

permitted them to interrupt the programme in progress, allowing Naujock's Polish-speaking announcers to broadcast anti-German statements for the next five minutes to the background accompaniment of shots fired by other SS men. Having decided they had convinced the listeners that the radio station was under attack by armed Poles, Naujocks and his men withdrew.

A successful mock attack on the German customs station at Hochlinden was also made by Heydrich's SS detachment. Here again concentration camp victims dressed in Polish uniforms were scattered around. Hitler had his justification for invading Poland. In fact his troops and tanks were on the move before the SS men had even returned to their bases.

On 1 September the incident at Gleiwitz was reported by the *Völkisher Beobachter*, the Nazi party's newspaper and mouthpiece, as being 'clearly the signal for a general attack on German territory by Polish guerrillas'.

On the morning of 1 September Hitler mounted the rostrum in the Kroll Opera House to announce to a hushed parliament that Germany was at war with Poland, declaring towards the end of his speech, 'From now on I am just the first soldier of the German Reich. I have once more put on the coat that was the most sacred and dear to me. I will not take it off again until victory is secured, or I will not survive the outcome.' His audience noticed that Hitler had discarded his customary brown Nazi Party jacket for a field-grey uniform blouse resembling that of an officer in the Waffen-SS.

The secret operation at Gleiwitz was only one of many attributed to the SS, but it will always be remembered as the one that spawned World War II. Hitler had two main agendas for world domination, one military and the other social, and the SS was to play an important and ever-growing part in each. At a meeting of his Wehrmacht commanders less than a fortnight before the invasion of Poland he had warned that 'things would be done of which German generals would not approve'.

Polish Blitzkrieg

The short war against Poland, the campaign that was over in 36 days, did not put a serious strain on the German war machine. The contribution of the SS-Verfügungstruppe was modest but not negligible. The SS-Totenkopfverbände on the other hand made no tactical contribution to the German victory, but was extensively involved in the Führer's social plan for Poland.

Himmler and Hitler were both keen to see the SS receive its baptism of fire in the Polish campaign. The army was by no means impressed with the military potential of Himmler's elite, still regarding

it with considerable discomfiture interwoven with much suspicion. During the attack, Himmler and his SS-Verfügungstruppe commanders had hoped that the SS-Verfügungstruppe would be deployed as a single formation. In an attempt to appease the army's disquiet, and much to Himmler's irritation, the Führer decided that the SS force should be split among army units to which it would be subordinated. During the summer of 1939 the major portion of the SS-Verfügungstruppe that had been shipped to East Prussia was organised into regimental combat groups and attached to larger army formations.

The Panzer Division *Kempf* had the *Deutschland*, the SS-Aufklärungs Abteilung reconnaissance detachment and the SS-Nachrichtensturmbann signals company attached to it. The division under the command of Major General Werner Kempf was deployed as part of I Corps in General Fedor von Bock's Army Group North.

The 10th Army, under General Walther von Reichenau, had the *SS-Leibstandarte* and the SS-Pioniersturmbann allocated to it, while the SS-Standarte *Germania* was retained in reserve in East Prussia as part of 14th Army. The third SS Standarte *Der Führer* which had been formed by SS-Obersturmbannführer Georg Keppler on 23 March 1938 was not yet fully trained and consequently did not take part in the Polish campaign. It found its duties in September lay in manning a section of the German West Wall defences on the Oberrheim-Front Breisach-Freiburg, under the command of 7th Army.

The Free City of Danzig had its own Allgemeine-SS unit, created to conduct operations of a 'police nature' in and around Danzig. The Danzig Senate had allowed the formation of a Volunteer Home Defence Force and imported arms

from East Prussia in response to Polish threats and killings in Danzig. It was organised as SS-Totenkopfsturmbann *Götze* in the spring of 1939, but was renamed SS-Heimwehr *Danzig* in July 1939, and reorganised into a reinforced infantry battalion under the command of SS-Obersturmbannführer Götze. The SS-Heimwehr *Danzig*, or SS Home Defence Regiment, was located in the Free City of Danzig and affiliated to the SS-Totenkopfverbände. It was sent into action under army command and used to help secure the port of Danzig and its environs. On

8 September the battalion shot 33 Polish civilians in the village of Hohenkirk in the province of Pomerania. In October 1939 it was incorporated into the *SS-Totenkopf* Division as the nucleus of the artillery regiment.

Action at Mlava

SS-Standartenführer Felix Steiner, leading *Deutschland*, struck south in the direction of Mlava, baked by hot searing sun and marching through dusty terrain. Despite the difficult conditions good progress was initially made, though the motorised capabilities could not be

fully utilised due to fuel shortages. The Polish positions were strongly constructed at the approaches to Mlava and manned by determined troops. Polish resistance began to stiffen quite considerably and this led to *Deutschland*'s first important engagement. Major General Kempf decided to prepare a formal attack with artillery and air support when the momentum of the German advance began to falter in front of a Polish bunker system. After a heavy and prolonged softening-up barrage by German artillery which proved less destructive than had been hoped, a two-pronged thrust against

Above: SS horse-drawn artillery on the move in western Poland in early September 1939. By this stage of the war only the Leibstandarte *Regiment was fully motorised among the military SS units. Regarding the German Army as a whole, it depended on horses for over 80 per cent of its motive power.*

the Polish defences was ordered, which *Deutschland* undertook, supported by tanks from 7th Panzer Regiment. The tank attack faltered almost immediately when they began to run into well prepared anti-tank obstacles. The German tanks, which comprised mainly light

Right: SS troops pause for a rest during the advance on Modlin in mid-September 1939. Note the white cross painted on the hull of the armoured fighting vehicle, a practice that was soon discontinued as it was discovered they made excellent aim marks for enemy anti-tank gunners. The mood in the picture is very relaxed.

Panzer I and Panzer II models, were insufficiently powerful to break through the defences. Polish artillery zeroed in on them and was able to wreak havoc, with the outcome that the panzers began to take heavy casualties. The remaining panzers were pulled back, as the attack could clearly not proceed. The promised Luftwaffe's Stuka dive-bomber attacks also failed to appear, making the situation untenable. The result was that some 39 tanks were either destroyed, damaged or disabled. Now, more or less alone, the *Deutschland* infantry could not succeed in pressing home their attack to drive out the Poles, in spite of their determination. Before being pulled back the SS infantry was able to get within nearly 100m (327ft) of the enemy bunkers.

Advance to the Narew

To the east at Chorzele an entire Polish corps was in full retreat. To pursue the fleeing Poles and press home this success Panzer Division *Kempf* was rushed forwards.

SS-Standartenführer Felix Steiner and SS-Standartenführer Matthais Kleinheisterkamp commanded SS battle groups which were supported by a battle group from 7th Panzer Regiment. In this new advance the Poles were swiftly driven back all the way to the River Narew. Here they formed new defence lines at Rozan in the network of four old czarist Russian forts. The Poles vigorously defended them, receiving many casualties, while the Germans' losses were considerable, rendering the infantry battalions from

Deutschland too weak to extricate the remaining Poles from their positions. The matter was decided with the appearance of Polish cavalry, and the Germans were forced to withdraw. During the engagement, 11 German tanks were lost to enemy gunfire and approximately 20 had been rendered unserviceable due to mechanical breakdown.

The Polish success was short-lived. Further to the south German forces had crossed the Narew and to avoid being encircled the Poles were forced to evacuate Rozan. The retreating Poles were pursued towards the River Bug by *Deutschland*, which captured Czervin and

Nadbory on the way. A strong Polish counterattack launched from Lomza to the north temporarily put *Deutschland* on the defensive but these attacks were beaten off with the help of 7th Panzer Regiment.

The Bug had been crossed by 10 September in an attempt to prevent Polish units strengthening the defences around Warsaw. Panzer Division *Kempf* was then ordered to drive south. Its route took it much further south, capturing Kaloszym, Siedlce and Zelechow before turning eastwards towards Najiejowice.

On 16 September Warsaw was completely encircled when SS-Standartefführer Kleinheisterkamp and his battle group reached the Vistula, closing the ring round the Polish capital. Desperate to prevent the fall of their capital city, determined Polish units had constantly harried the German forces, making it a costly albeit successful advance.

Germania's war

The Polish forts at Modlin and Zacrozym were next to be attacked. Modlin had a force to be reckoned with, holding approximately 35,000 troops that could be counted on to undertake a fanatical defence. To enable it to take part in the attack *Deutschland* found itself moved to the northwest of Warsaw.

Heavy losses were suffered by the patrols reconnoitring the Polish positions. These, however, were seriously weakened by several days of attacks by Stukas, and the Polish defences were stormed by SS troops in a final assault on 29 September. Zacrozym was stormed after an artillery barrage; within 90 minutes the fort was captured and several thousand prisoners taken.

During the night of 16–17 August, SS Regiment *Germania*, under the command of SS-Standartenführer Carl-Maria Demelhuber, was brought together at Königsbrück training area near Dresden in preparation for the Polish campaign. It was then placed under the command of 14th Army, with its armoured car platoon serving under the 8th Reconnaissance Unit of the 8th Armoured Division. Although *Germania* remained in reserve for most of the four-week campaign, it was assigned the task of protecting the flank of XXII Army

Corps in its drive towards Chelm as part of 10th Army attacking from Silesia. Elements of *Germania* guarding the flanks of XXII Army Corps were too weak, as they were too thinly spread on the ground. The regiment, in fact, was broken down into sub-units and allocated to various army units. The VIII Army Corps received the 2nd Battalion, the 5th Panzer Division took the Armoured Reconnaissance Platoon, and 2 and 3 Companies were held in reserve.

The task of blocking the Przemysl–Lemberg road fell to 15 Company. Here the SS infantry surprised a Polish column of approximately battalion size and, despite being vastly outnumbered, managed to take over 500 prisoners. Officers and cadets from the Polish War Academy at Kraców, who had been formed into a powerful unit, were attempting to fight their way through to Lemberg on the evening of the same day, when they ran into the small SS unit. The Germans took heavy casualties and were forced to withdraw to the north to link up with 1 Company. The SS troops were ordered to hold their positions despite the perilous situation. Przemysl was under attack from the 7th Infantry Division and they succeeded in stopping any Polish troops from escaping.

The regiment's 2nd Battalion, attached to the 8th Infantry Division of VIII Army Corps, advanced towards the line Brzoza–Stadnice–Linica. At Kreszov there was a vital bridge over the River San, which had to be captured intact, and this became the battalion's initial task. To keep to the attack timetable a gruelling march of around 80km (49 miles) over just two days was required. Elements of the 5th Panzer Division were encountered en route by the battalion and together they pushed their way forward, reaching the west bank of the San on 12 September. However, the bridge was blown up just as the Germans were preparing to cross. One platoon each from 3 Company and 5 Company crossed the river that night, only to find that under the cover of darkness the Poles had withdrawn. The fleeing Poles were pursued by 6 Company, which came so close at times that the Stukas harrying the retreat were in danger of hitting SS troops. The San's eastern banks had been secured by the time the 8th Infantry Division arrived.

The 10th Army under General Walther von Reichenau had the *Leibstandarte* attached to it, commanded by SS-Gruppenführer 'Sepp' Dietrich together with elements of

Right: Closely following the German Army columns marching into Poland came the SS death squads, tasked by Reinhard Heydrich, the head of the SS's security service, to search out and annihilate all 'undesirables'. This meant Jews, communists and members of the Polish intelligentsia were rounded up and shot.

the SS-Pioniersturmbann. It was deployed in the central sector and was assigned the task of protecting the exposed flanks of the Wehrmacht units that were racing ahead. As a fully motorised regiment the *Leibstandarte* was particularly suited to this function, showing its value particularly in respect of the 17th Infantry Division as it drove towards the area west of the Polish capital.

The 4th Panzer Division advanced towards Lodz and the *Leibstandarte* was now transferred to support it. Initially everything in its path was easily swept aside, but the further it advanced into the heartland the stiffer the opposition became. In large towns vicious street fighting often bogged the regiment down and in particular there was a case in the town of Pabianice where determined Polish units surrounded the SS men. The beleaguered

Leibstandarte was only relieved by the intervention of army troops.

The 4th Army and 10th Army pincer movement began to be executed, and to the west of Warsaw vast numbers of Polish troops were cut off as the Germans closed in on the capital. The German strategists had assumed that these Polish units would attempt to withdraw eastwards, but in fact they struck south. The *Leibstandarte* was now attached to the 8th Army and on 10 September these Polish units went straight into its exposed flank and smashed at it for two days until their attacks began to lose momentum. Finally they had to turn east in the hope of reaching Warsaw. The next move the *Leibstandarte* made was westwards, taking part in the encirclement on the River Bzura.

The Polish campaign is often seen only in the light of the German

Above: Polish prisoners are escorted from the post office in the so-called Free City of Danzig by members of the SS-Heimwehr Danzig, a Totenkopf home defence force, after their valiant efforts to fight off the Germans at the beginning of 1939. As a foretaste of things to come, most of these men were shot by the SS.

invasion, but in truth a great part of the successes of the action were due to the part played by the Soviet intervention. This was not just military but also the psychological part it played on the Poles.

The Polish government and high command and indeed the German High Command were taken completely by surprise when just before dawn on 17 September the Soviet Union entered the war. The Red Army crossed the border along its entire length from the Dzwina to the Dniestr, some 1280km (790 miles).

Although resistance still continued, the fight was hopeless with the entry of Soviet troops into Poland. The main Polish aim was now to get as many fighting personnel out of the country as possible, so that they could continue the fight on the side of the Allies. German and Soviet troops concentrated on cutting off the Polish retreat to Rumania and Hungary and met on 20 September on the upper Dniestr.

Only those Polish troops on or near the Rumanian bridgehead managed to get across the border; in all, 30,000 Polish soldiers and airmen reached Rumania and 60,000 crossed into Hungary. In the north, Soviet troops pushed about 15,000 Polish soldiers to the Lithuanian and Latvian borders. In the centre the Germans tried and failed to beat the Soviets to Lwow and its oil fields. Polish troops from the Chelm-Lublin area and from eastern Malopolska were trying to fight through to the Hungarian frontier but their attempts were thwarted, forcing them to capitulate, some to German and others to the Soviet troops.

Poland capitulates

Meanwhile, Warsaw, surrounded but still fighting, was repulsing German attacks while trying to help Polish troops to break through. On 25 September, however, the Germans began the decisive assault. During 26–27 September, with strong air and artillery support, they attacked on all sectors on both sides of the Vistula. The attacks were mainly repulsed but with food and ammunition running out, the city was forced to capitulate. On 29 September the fortress at Modlin followed suit. Fighting on the Baltic and Polish shores ended on 1 October when the Polish naval commander surrendered. The fighting on land had been particularly bloody with an extremely gallant Polish resistance, but on 6 October the last Polish troops ceased fighting.

German casualties, according to their October 1939 estimate, were 8082 killed, 27,279 wounded and 5029 missing, although the final figures were slightly higher. German tank losses were 217 destroyed and a large number damaged, while the Luftwaffe lost 285 aircraft destroyed and 279 damaged beyond repair – in all about 25 per cent of the aircraft used. Polish casualties cannot be accurately assessed but were much higher and also included civilians. Poland lost 284 aircraft in combat and 149 for other reasons.

Below: All smiles for these SS members at the conclusion of the Polish Campaign. The country had been conquered in a lightning assault and armed SS units had performed well. The army complained that SS units had been too reckless. No matter, Hitler was impressed, and authorised an expansion of Himmler's legions.

CHAPTER 3

BLITZKRIEG IN THE WEST

In recognition of its sterling service in Poland, Hitler agreed to the formation of three new SS divisions prior to the 1940 campaign in the West, a campaign in which the Waffen-SS would once again display great courage on the battlefield. Himmler's soldiers showed themselves to be masters at the all-arms battle.

Left: Members of the Totenkopf *Division with their 37mm Pak 35/36 anti-tank gun in action in France in May 1940. Initially in the reserve, the division was rushed to the front in mid-May.*

Right: Soldiers of the Totenkopf *Division about to cross a river under fire in France in May 1940. The division had first gone into action to relieve pressure on Erwin Rommel's 7th Panzer Division, losing 16 dead and 53 wounded while attacking towards Le Cateau and Cambrai. Its men were fanatical in the attack.*

The German Army now had a total of 10 panzer divisions with the formation of four new armoured divisions, which were employed with the important mobile forces, the spearhead of Blitzkrieg operations. The Wehrmacht, though, was under-strength with regard to support for the armoured forces, still having only the four motorised infantry divisions it possessed the previous September when the war began. The *SS-Verfügungs* Division, *Totenkopf* Division and the reinforced regiment *Leibstandarte SS Adolf Hitler* were employed to make up the shortfall. In all, the Waffen-SS countered the deficiency by supplying the equivalent of three divisions of motorised infantry, and by the launch of the offensive in the West it had more than 125,000 men in uniform, counting the personnel of the *SS-Totenkopf* regiments, the non-motorised *Polizei* Division and replacements in training.

Attitude of the army

The task of the SS field commander was complicated by a number of factors, including the attitude of individual army commanders, which was often less than cordial towards the SS. The older established SS regiments, which had previously served under army command and had fought in Poland, *Leibstandarte*, *Deutschland*, *Germania* and, to a lesser extent, *Der Führer*, which had not, were treated with healthy respect. Paul Hausser, Felix Steiner and 'Sepp' Dietrich, who commanded them, were respected, or at least accepted, by their army colleagues.

What little the army field commanders had heard about Himmler's two newest divisions and their commanding officers hardly seemed reassuring, conjoined with the fact that they had not yet proved themselves in battle. A police general, SS-Gruppenführer und Generalleutnant der Polizei Karl von Pfeffer-Wildenbruch, led the *Polizei* Division, which consisted of former members of the Ordnungspolizei or the ordinary police armed with Czech weapons, supported by vintage horse-drawn artillery and transport; hardly the most inspiring combination. Himmler's supervisor of concentration camps, SS-Gruppenführer Theodor Eicke, commanded the *Totenkopf* Division, which comprised political fanatics as well as a sizeable number of former concentration camp guards.

The *Totenkopf* Division

Himmler did not object when *Polizei* Division was assigned a passive defence role opposite the Maginot Line for Fall Gelbe. The concentration camp guards, however, were another matter. Himmler saw an opportunity to demonstrate that *Totenkopf* Division was as capable of engaging in the honourable pro-

he was told that a heavy artillery section was being organised for the division, and he completed his tour in a frame of mind that differed from that in which he had arrived. On a second visit, he expressed himself most pleased by the SS troops' superb physical condition after observing a rapid mock assault using live fire.

The Western Campaign of 1940 was a milestone in the development of the Waffen-SS, as for the first time SS troops fought in divisional formations under the command of their own officers. The combat forces of the SS were at full strength by the end of April 1940, and despite some shortages in artillery and transport, were ready for battle. Their performance assured the Waffen-SS a permanent place as the de facto fourth branch of the Wehrmacht. It was during May and June 1940 in the campaigns in Holland and France that the Waffen-SS began to acquire the reputation that in later years made it the hope of its Führer and the despair of its foes.

The campaign begins

Hitler finally decided on 9 May that the attack westward would begin the following day. At 2100 hours that evening the code word 'Danzig' was given, signalling the launching of Fall Gelbe. The 139 divisions, three of which were SS, plus one SS regiment, the *Leibstandarte*, were marshalled for the offensive and divided into the Army Groups B, A and C. They were deployed in that order along a 640km (396-mile) front that spread from northern Holland to the Swiss border. Army Group B was commanded by General Fedor von Bock and consisted of 29 divisions. Army Group A, commanded by General Gerd von Rundstedt, was to undertake the task of the Schwerpunkt, or point of main effort. His impressive force consisted of 45 divisions and included the bulk of

fession of soldiering as the dreaded Death's Head units were of brutalising helpless prisoners in the concentration camps. He considered this a matter of honour and prestige, which made him press strongly for the inclusion of *Totenkopf* Division in the crucial first-wave attack. However, it had already been concluded by General Franz Halder, chief of the Army General Staff, that the division would find 'a battle of weapons a difficult undertaking'. In the end General von Weich's 2nd Army was assigned the *Totenkopf* Division, forming a part of the OKH reserve that was to follow the lead

German divisions into Belgium and Luxembourg.

The commander of the 2nd Army, General Maximilian Freiherr von Weichs, was one of the army's senior field commanders, an aristocrat and a devout Catholic. He undertook his first visit to *Totenkopf* Division on 4 April and made no effort to hide the fact he was not favourably inclined towards the SS. Eicke described the general's manner upon his arrival as 'cold and hostile' (Weichs had been told that the division was not motorised and was of inferior quality in general). However, his professional interest was stimulated when

the German armour. Three powerful echelons and densely packed panzer corps, containing approximately 2000 tanks, were to lead. The entire OKH reserve of 45 divisions, including the 2nd Army and the *Totenkopf* Division, were assigned as a back-up force exclusively for Army Group A. Army Group C was commanded by General Wilhelm Ritter von Leeb and could only boast a modest force of 19 infantry divisions. Army Groups A and B, assisted by a division of airborne troops, were to carry out the campaign Fall Gelbe entirely on their own. Army Group C was given no active role in the first part of the campaign. Its static divisions were to stand fast opposite the Maginot Line, with the exception of a feinting attack in the Saar region.

The German plan called for three main attacks by about 75 divisions, with 45 in reserve. The objective of the northernmost attack was to crush the Dutch defences and occupy Holland. Dutch airfields would then be denied to the RAF. This attack was to be delivered by a section of Army Group B, while the remaining and more powerful portion of the army group was to push into the heart of Belgium. It was hoped that the two attacks would lure the allies northward. Army Group A would deliver the main strike, thrusting a wedge through southern Belgium and Luxembourg and into northern France. The Dutch and Belgian armies would be swept aside and the encirclement and destruction of the British Expeditionary Force – the BEF – and a part of the French Army would be achieved. Fall Rot – Case Red – would then be implemented, a southward movement of all German forces into France to crush the remaining French forces.

When the final dispositions were completed the *Leibstandarte SS Adolf Hitler* and the 3rd Regiment *Der Führer*, now detached from the *Verfügungs* Division, stood poised on the Dutch frontier. The remainder of the *Verfügungs* Division was on alert near Münster, ready to move into Holland as soon as the border defences had been breached. The *Verfügungs* Division was held in OKH reserve near Kassel and the *Polizei* Division was in reserve at Tübingen behind the Upper Rhine front of Army Group C.

Below: Totenkopf vehicles near Arras on 21 May 1940 (note the divisional death's head symbol on the vehicle on the right). The British armoured counterattack near Arras was a sobering experience for Eicke's men, and was halted only because of the reckless courage displayed by the Waffen-SS soldiers.

The role the SS units were to play in the campaign were to be vigorous; the *Leibstandarte* and *Der Führer* Regiments were deployed as part of the first wave of 18th Army in Army Group B. Their objective was to seize rail and road bridges over the Dutch border. A second wave that encompassed the remainder of the *Verfügungs* Division was tasked with forcing crossings over the Dutch border further south.

Holland defeated

As dawn broke on 10 May 1940, the *Leibstandarte* overpowered Dutch border guards and by midday had covered 100km (62 miles), capturing Zarolle, where the Dutch Army had demolished the bridge over the River Yssel. Undeterred, the SS troops constructed improvised rafts. They then pushed forward a further 80km (50 miles) that day, but more

importantly their objective of securing a crossing over the Yssel had been achieved. On the drive towards Rotterdam the *Leibstandarte* then turned south to link up with elements of the *Verfügungs* Division.

The advance near Arnhem of the 227th Infantry Division was spearheaded by *Der Führer* Regiment, which crossed the Yssel near the town. The Dutch had destroyed all the suitable bridges in this sector, but a bridgehead on the west bank had been established by the 2nd Battalion, which had forced a crossing. Temporary bridges were soon erected by SS Pioneers, allowing the 3rd Battalion to surge across and enter Arnhem, which fell around mid-day. The Dutch had counted on the natural defence line offered by the Yssel to help them hold the Germans for at least three days, when in reality it held for just four

Above: Waffen-SS infantry on the attack near Dunkirk towards the end of May 1940. By the end of the month the Leibstandarte, along with other German Army units, was closing in on the British Expeditionary Force around the port. On 30 May it was withdrawn from the front and went into the reserve for a refit.

hours. *Der Führer* burst through the Grebbe Line, the next line of Dutch defences, the following day.

So pleased were X Corps with the performance of *Der Führer* Regiment that it was now entrusted with a lead role in the headlong rush across Holland. *Der Führer* finished its drive on the coast at Zandvoort as the pell-mell advance continued. Here and there a spirited defence had been put up by Dutch troops, but the unstoppable momentum of the SS soon swept them aside. News that the Dutch were prepared to

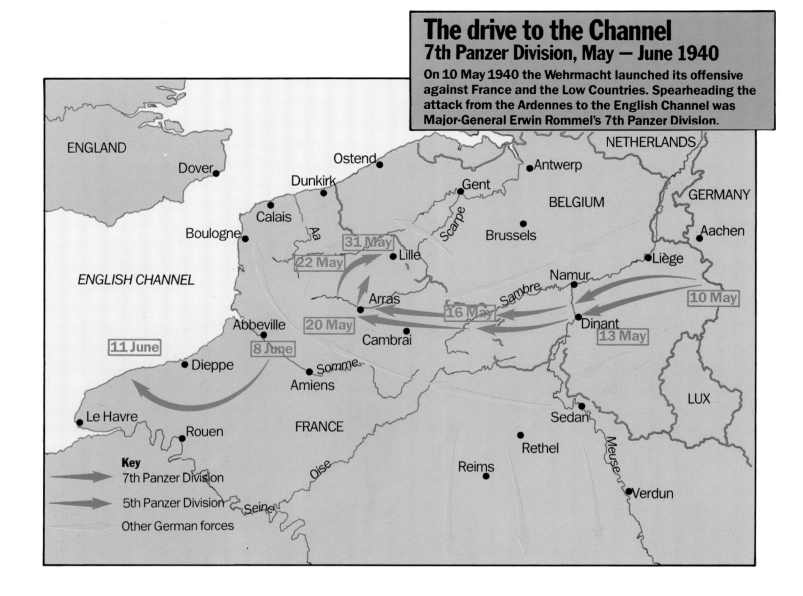

The drive to the Channel
7th Panzer Division, May — June 1940
On 10 May 1940 the Wehrmacht launched its offensive against France and the Low Countries. Spearheading the attack from the Ardennes to the English Channel was Major-General Erwin Rommel's 7th Panzer Division.

Key
7th Panzer Division
5th Panzer Division
Other German forces

surrender Rotterdam failed to reach the Luftwaffe command. This led to one of the great tragedies of the campaign, for on 12 May 1940 the Luftwaffe indiscriminately bombed Rotterdam, leaving the city devastated. General Dietrich von Choltiz and General Kurt Student of the Luftwaffe paratroop forces were in the city later that day negotiating the surrender when advance elements of the *Leibstandarte* raced into the city square. Dutch soldiers were standing aimlessly outside the building in which the negotiations were being conducted. Without hesitation the SS troops opened fire, and in the confusion a stray German bullet hit and seriously wounded General Kurt Student. Heading

towards Delft, the *Leibstandarte* pressed onwards and took 4000 Dutch prisoners. The Dutch Army was on the verge of capitulating by the time they reached the Hague, and here the War Ministry was occupied and the garrison disarmed. They were just in time to witness the Dutch surrender on 14 May.

The 18th Army's south flank was being covered against potential attacks by the Allied units striking north out of France by the bulk of the *Verfügungs* Division, which had been advancing towards the area north of Antwerp. The division was permitted to move south into Belgium when these attacks failed to materialise. Just south of Rotterdam the vital Moerdijk Bridges had

Above: Rommel's 7th Panzer Division was one of the Wehrmacht's first-rate units. Its dash to the English Channel in 1940 established the reputation of its commander. However, things might have been different had it not have been for the Totenkopf *steadying the 7th's nerves during the British attack at Arras.*

by this time been captured by German paratroops and a French relief force was dispatched to drive them out. The advance elements of 9th Panzer Division, to which the *Leibstandarte* was temporarily attached, collided with part of the French relief force, resulting in a ferocious fight from which the French were forced to withdraw. Fresh orders had been received by the *Verfügungs* Division, directing it to attack towards the coast, with the objective of capturing the heavily defended Walcheren and Beveland islands. These islands would have to be taken by storm, for although the Dutch had surrendered on 14 May, the Allied troops deployed on them refused to capitulate. This was a daunting undertaking as they were supported by Royal Navy ships lying off the coast and also by artillery fire from around Antwerp.

First action for the *Totenkopf*

The sheer size of the German break-through and the surprising speed of the advances on 15–16 May startled even senior German commanders and dictated the call-up of reserves to fill the gaps and protect the flanks of the rapidly widening armoured salient.

Accordingly, on 16 May the *Totenkopf* Division received orders to go into action with General Hoth's XV Panzer Corps. This comprised 5th and 7th Panzer Divisions, which formed the northern cutting edge of the German spearhead as part of Army Group A. Just before dawn on the morning of 18 May Eicke moved out in his command car, leading his entire division, assembled into marching columns. The division motored west from Neukirchen to Roermund in Holland where they took the road towards Belgium, which now led them in a southerly direction. On reaching Maastricht the *Totenkopf* continued southwest, detouring to Liège in the south and pushing through Huy towards Dinant. Eicke's columns

Right: The charismatic, if blunt, commander of the Leibstandarte: *'Sepp' Dietrich. A personal friend of Hitler, he won the Knight's Cross for leading it in France. It was nearly a posthumous decoration, as Dietrich had been nearly killed by the British after becoming separated from his command while near Dunkirk in May.*

encountered no resistance on their advance through Holland and Belgium as by 18 May the British and French had been pushed further to the west by Bock's army group.

While Eicke was pausing to rest near the French border at 0400 hours on 19 May, he received intelligence that counterattacks in regimental strength were imminent from the north and that he should prepare his command. Orders from

XV Panzer Corps followed shortly afterwards, requiring the division to move into France and proceed as quickly as possible to the village of Le Cateau. The 7th Panzer Division commanded by Major-General Erwin Rommel had been pinned down by a savage French counter-attack between Le Cateau and Cambrai. It now fell to the *Totenkopf* to rescue one of the army's crack divisions. Eicke ordered an attack

Above: Time for a photograph during the Western Campaign. Note the SS designation on the truck's number plate. The German plan for Case Red, the conquest of France, was issued by OKH on 31 May. Its aim was to 'annihilate the Allied forces still remaining in France', an order the SS eagerly participated in.

across the River Sambre towards both Le Cateau and Cambrai to relieve the pressure on Rommel, assigning the *Totenkopf* Division's 1st Infantry Regiment and anti-tank, engineer and artillery companies for the mission.

In their first contact with the enemy, Eicke's men encountered French Moroccan troops. In a day-long engagement they methodically cleared the Mojos in vicious hand-to-hand fighting from several small villages. The SS troops then had to repulse a series of tank attacks. The area east and north of Cambrai had been cleared of enemy forces by Eicke's men by mid-morning on 20 May and the XV Panzer Corps was now free to resume its advance that afternoon. Units of the *Totenkopf* Division captured four majors, two colonels, 1600 soldiers and a large cache of weapons and supplies during this first engagement.

On the afternoon of 21 May a force of around 74 British tanks and two battalions of infantry supported by an additional 60 tanks belonging to the French 3rd Light Mechanised Division slammed into the flanks of the advancing 7th Panzer and *Totenkopf* Divisions. The Allied armour, particularly the 30-tonne (30-ton) British Matildas, may have been slow, cumbersome and poorly armed, but their very thick plating proved to be a more than adequate match for the 37mm anti-tank guns. The SS anti-tank troops were horrified to find their shells bouncing off the enemy tanks unless they fired at point-blank range. Heavy losses were inflicted by the Matildas, especially upon the 3rd Company of the tank destroyer battalion. Some gun crews were crushed beneath the Matildas' relentless tracks or blasted to smithereens at close range.

After nearly an hour of desperate resistance, Eicke managed to stall the attack by firing over open sights on the British with artillery provided by Rommel. He moved his 88mm anti-aircraft guns up and deployed them in the anti-tank role, as these were the only German anti-tank gun capable of destroying a Matilda at the time. The Allied force destroyed nine German medium tanks, a number of light tanks and a large amount of motor transport, and inflicted casualties of 89 killed, 116 wounded and 173 missing. This assault, the stiffest *Totenkopf* Division had encountered, cost the Allies 39 dead, 66 wounded and two missing.

Hoepner's rage

The *Totenkopf* Division pressed onwards towards Merville, suffering such high casualties that General Erich Hoepner of the 7th Panzer Division went to Bethune where he might examine the situation at close hand. Hoepner was strongly opposed to the SS and had doubts about the *Totenkopf* Division's reliability in particular. Apparently Eicke had challenged the halt and withdrawal order he had previously received. The meeting between the two men was tense, and a spluttering Eike told Hoepner that losses made no difference when one held a position and the SS did not retreat in the face of the enemy. Hoepner, visibly angered, reprimanded Eicke sharply in front of his own staff, accusing him of caring nothing for the lives of his men, and even allegedly calling him a 'butcher'.

On 22 May an order was given to the 6th and 8th Panzer Divisions and the *Verfügungs* Division to strike with all possible speed towards Calais. A French force of approximately battalion strength was stunned by the appearance of a 30-man reconnaissance troop in their midst and immediately surrendered. This one action illustrates the volatility of this hectic advance, though the *Verfügungs* Division itself was soon to run into trouble, coming under attack from heavily armoured French tanks.

By 24 May the *Leibstandarte*, attached to the 1st Panzer Division, was in position by the Aa Canal and poised for the push on Dunkirk. An area roughly triangular in shape now held the Allies. It was situated between Terneuzen in the north, Valenciennes in the south and Gravelines in the southwest. A line of canals which formed natural defence lines ran along the southern flank of the triangle where the British defenders were located on high ground on the opposite bank, giving them a view of the area, including the *Leibstandarte*'s positions opposite Watten.

News arrived the same day of Hitler's Führerbefehl or 'leader's command' in which he gave the 'halt order' which stunned Dietrich, the *Leibstandarte*'s commander. His men, exposed to the British observers, were now coming under heavy artillery fire, and were preparing their assault over the canal. Dietrich decided to ignore the Führerbefehl and ordered his men to continue the planned attack. The *Leibstandarte* stormed over the canal and succeeded in capturing the heights.

Before the halt order was received, the canal in a nearby sector had been crossed by one of the *Verfügungs* Division's reconnaissance patrols, which managed to penetrate 8km (five miles) behind the enemy defence lines before being intercepted. The defence of

this part of the canal was weak and the division immediately dispatched an assault force to establish a bridgehead on the opposite bank.

Meanwhile, an order was given to the *Verfügungs* Division to drive the British forces out of the Forêt de Nieppe. The Germans prepared for a long battle, finding the British resistance resolute. However the Belgians surrendered, leaving the British with an exposed flank, which caused a tactical withdrawal. This

Below: The strain begins to show for these two Waffen-SS soldiers during the Battle of France in June 1940. While the Leibstandarte *took part in the spearhead of the Blitzkrieg, the other Waffen-SS divisions followed well behind the panzers, undertaking the more mundane tasks of guarding flanks and reducing pockets.*

was accomplished methodically, with great cost to the Germans.

Hitler's 'halt order' was lifted on the night of 26–27 May. At Bethune the *Totenkopf* crossed the canal and pushed towards Merville. British troops put up determined resistance and the *Totenkopf* suffered significant casualties at their hands.

Taking the Lys Canal

Meanwhile, the *Deutschland* Regiment, in company with the army's 3rd Panzer Division, was also pushing towards Merville. On 27 May the SS troops reached the Lys Canal, where they encountered British defence lines. German artillery laid down a softening-up barrage, then SS-Oberführer Felix Steiner ordered an attack across the canal. The 3rd Battalion was thrown across and the British defenders driven out. By that evening a bridgehead had been established by two full battalions of SS troops, which had crossed by the afternoon. However, this was to be a short-lived success; the British still held the area on both flanks and the *Totenkopf* Division's support was still some way behind. A fierce British tank assault suddenly hit Steiner's troops. The British armour was driven off but artillery fire continued to rain down on the German positions, preventing chase being given to the retreating British.

To the north, the *Leibstandarte* continued its drive on Dunkirk and the Dunkirk perimeter, which held within it thousands of men of the BEF, awaiting evacuation. On 28 May 1940 the commanding officer, 'Sepp' Dietrich, received orders to attack the village of Wormhoudt, which lay between Kassel and Dunkirk and was held by men of the British 48th Division and in particular the 2nd Royal Warwicks, and machine-gunners of the 4th Cheshire Regiment. Later that day, near Esquebeck, Dietrich and his adjutant, Max Wünsche, were on a forward

recce when their vehicle was raked by gunfire. A drainage ditch afforded the SS officers cover but they were pinned down. Leaking fuel was ignited and the two men, in danger of being incinerated, covered themselves with mud in an attempt to fend off the flames. Two companies were dispatched to extricate them from the ditch but they were beaten back. A tank platoon made a further attempt, which also failed. A force finally worked its way around the British and attacked from the rear.

The size of the force required for Dietrich and Wünsche to be rescued

Above: A Waffen-SS recruiting poster. In 1939 the armed SS had consisted of around 28,000 men. However, before the war was a year old, its strength had risen to 150,000, due in no small measure to Gottlob Berger, who established a nationwide SS recruiting network. Volksdeutsche (ethnic Germans) were also recruited.

illustrates the ferocity of the fighting between the British and SS troops. Enraged in the belief that their revered commander had been killed, the *Leibstandarte* hurled themselves at the Wormhoudt defences. Resistance was determined and when the

Leibstandarte finally secured the village it had to repulse fierce counterattacks.

On 30 May, the *Leibstandarte* was withdrawn and placed in reserve in the Cambrai region, where it enjoyed a brief period of rest and was refitted. The *Verfügungs* Division joined it there, while on 31 May the *Totenkopf* division was deployed south of the Dunkirk perimeter on coastal security duties.

The conquest of France

By early June the British forces in the north had been eliminated, so all three German army groups turned south. Army Group B advanced on a line from the River Aisne to the coast, Army Group A from the Franco-German border to the River Aisne and Army Group C attacked through the Maginot Line. Just 65 French formations were arrayed

against about 140 German divisions. Rested, strengthened by replacements from Germany and fully refitted, the SS units were ready for action. On 5 June Army Group B, including Panzer Group *Kleist*, with the *Leibstandarte* and the *Verfügungs* Division attached, began its drive towards Paris.

Encountering only light resistance, the *Verfügungs* Division had crossed the River Somme by 6 June. French resistance stiffened, however, the nearer it drew to Paris and it came under concentrated French fire as it approached the River Aisne. The French, it became clear, would not give ground without a great struggle, although the *Der Führer* Regiment forced a crossing. As a result the SS troops were pulled back over the Somme and the line of their advance was moved further east.

On 10 June the French Government abandoned Paris, which was declared an open city on 12 June. The River Meuse was crossed at Château-Thierry by the *Leibstandarte* on 12 June. The *Totenkopf* Division was released from the reserve at this stage to participate in the advance. The French moved their main defence lines from the north of the capital to the south on 13 June. Sensing the imminent collapse of the French, the German High Command issued a directive on 14 June designed to conclude the

Below: A Polizei *Division field kitchen in France in June 1940. The division was composed of former policemen, was not motorised, and had second-rate equipment and weaponry. It was not surprising, therefore, that it performed badly during the campaign. After being mauled by the French it was withdrawn into the reserve.*

campaign. Hitler ordered 'a sharp pursuit' in the direction of Orléans to prevent the French from forming a new front south of Paris and the 'annihilation' of the remaining French forces along the eastern front. To assist in this operation, Army Group C was ordered to launch an immediate assault against the Maginot Line and the Rhine front.

To prevent any French units attempting to escape to the southwest, Panzer Group Kleist pushed through the Champagne region towards Dijon. The *Leibstandarte*, a fully motorised formation, was able to keep up with the spearhead of the advance, while the mopping-up operations were carried out by slower divisions which followed in their wake. Some 30,000 French prisoners were taken by the *Verfügungs* Division for the loss of just 33 of its own men.

The *Leibstandarte* raced on, smashing barricades with armoured cars and mortar fire and unblocking the roads. Forward units drove at top speed, taking on enemy forces with automatic weapons blazing from the moving vehicles. These lead elements bypassed occupied towns, leaving them to be vanquished by the following SS infantry battalions. 'Sepp' Dietrich's men excelled in this kind of fighting, and the *Leibstandarte* in this helter-skelter manner reached St Pourcain on 19 June. The same day Gannat was taken, while an intact bridge allowed the River Allier to be recrossed and a link-up at Vichy made with other German troops.

The race south

The hectic advance continued and Clermont-Ferrand was captured by the *Leibstandarte* on 20 June. It netted 242 aircraft after capturing the airfield along with eight tanks, one general, 286 officers and over 4075 men. Only 24 hours later, the *Leibstandarte* marched on St Etienne, where its garrison also surrendered.

The *Verfügungs* Division was still advancing, albeit more slowly than the *Leibstandarte*, protecting the open left flank from attacks by French units attempting to escape encirclement. But after its success in beating off the French breakout attempt of 16–17 June it had little to do and spent the rest of the week mopping up behind the *Leibstandarte* and the panzer divisions.

On the right flank the *Totenkopf* Division had even less to do. But much to Eicke's joy, on 19 June the division was at last committed with the forward elements of Panzer Group *Kleist* and given the mission of advancing some 140km (87 miles) to the south to Tarare. It then reconnoitred to Lyon. Even then the division did not see much action. Its reconnaissance squadron did, however, find itself in a furious battle with French colonial troops at Tarare, taking 6000 prisoners while suffering only light losses.

The Battle of France was to all intents and purposes finished for Hausser's and Eicke's SS divisions. On 9–10 June, the River Aisne and

Below: The Panzer III. This tank was the mainstay of the early Waffen-SS panzer regiments. It had a crew of five: driver, radio operator/machine gunner, gunner, loader and commander. It held its own up until the invasion of Russia in June 1941, when it came up against the T-34.

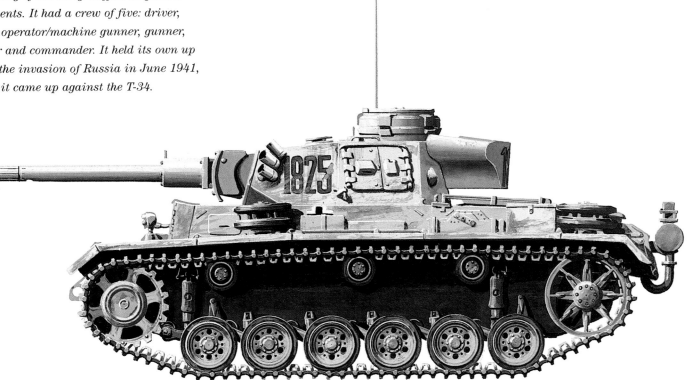

the Ardennes canal were crossed by the *Polizei* Division in the company of Army Group A. The German forces were then counterattacked by French armour and the battle raged with the balance swinging back and forth for some time, until eventually the French were overcome by the sheer weight of the German advance. The *Polizei* Division then advanced through the Argonne Forest. Here, in its second and last major engagement, undertaken in the Argonne Pass near Les Islettes, the division engaged with a French rearguard, equipped with heavy artillery. The French defended themselves with toughness, skill and lethal hand-to-hand combat but the 2nd Police Regiment finally broke through, capturing the town of Les Islettes. The *Polizei* Division continued to secure the left flank of the German advance but had no sig-

nificant contact with the enemy during this time.

The *Polizei* Division was withdrawn and sent into reserve once again on 20 June southwest of Bar le Duc. It had suffered casualties that amounted to a grand total of 707 men, seven officers and 125 men killed, 12 officers and 515 men wounded, and 48 men missing – a poor tally for what were two comparatively minor engagements

The performance of the Waffen-SS delighted Hitler, who once again expressed his unequivocal support. There could be no mistake that it had won its spurs, though its triumph had been marred by the all too familiar crop of atrocities which were becoming common among SS units (see Chapter 13). Five Knight's Crosses had been bestowed upon SS personnel as tangible proof of the Waffen-SS's heroism: SS-Ober-

Above: 'Sepp' Dietrich bestows honours on his men for their valour during the Western Campaign. The Waffen-SS in 1940 was a small but well equipped formation staffed by extremely fit soldiers who were motivated by Nazi ideology. They were, to use Adolf Hitler's words, 'the sense of superiority personified'.

gruppenführer Dietrich for his leadership of the Leibstandarte on 4 July 1940, SS-Oberführer Georg Keppler for his command of *Der Führer* Regiment, *Verfügungs* Division on 15 August 1940, SS-Oberführer Felix Steiner for his leadership of the *Deutschland* Regiment on the same day, SS-Obersturmführer Fritz Vogt, a platoon leader in the Reconnaissance Battalion of the *Verfügungs* Division, on 4 September 1940, and SS-Hauptscharführer Ludwig Kepplinger, 11 Company, *Der Führer* Regiment on 4 September 1940.

CHAPTER 4

BALKAN WHIRLWIND

The crushing of Yugoslavia and Greece in the spring of 1941 was a classic demonstration of the Blitzkrieg, and once again the Waffen-SS earned high praise for its actions, particularly the *Das Reich* Division. However, the conquest of the Balkans delayed the invasion of the Soviet Union by four weeks, which both the army and Waffen-SS would pay a heavy price for later when the Russian winter gripped the German forces on the Eastern Front.

Left: Leibstandarte *personnel engage Greek troops in April 1941 during the invasion of the Balkans. Note the divisional symbol on the hull of the Sd Kfz 222 light armoured car.*

In November 1940, Hitler formulated plans for a more effective invasion of Greece. The German plan, code-named Operation 'Marita', required the deployment of 16 divisions in bases in southern Rumania from which they would attack south. The initial concept was to seize the Greek mainland north of the Aegean Sea, but with the British intervention and the landing of troops in Greece early in March, the decision was made to occupy the whole peninsula, and the island of Crete. The objective now was to drive the British and Commonwealth troops out and force the Greeks to surrender.

The Tripartite Pact signed by Rome, Berlin, and Tokyo in 1940 was the cornerstone of the Axis, and to secure their allegiance Hungary, Romania, and Slovakia were all encouraged to join. Bulgaria followed in 1941 and on 25 March Yugoslavia followed the Bulgarian example and became a signatory, albeit under intense German diplomatic pressure. The route to the Greek border seemed assured.

The Waffen-SS moves east

However, at 0220 hours on 27 March the Yugoslav military revolted and the government fell. At dawn a radio proclamation declared that a new anti-German government was established.

In Britain there was jubilation in the War Cabinet, while across the Atlantic there was a quiet optimism. It was the reaction in Berlin, however, that was critical. The Germans had decided that they would assist the Italians to overcome the Greeks once spring thawed the Balkan roads. Now the snow was melting and Operation 'Marita' was to begin in the first week of April. More important, the invasion of Russia, Operation 'Barbarossa', was sched-

Above: Troops of the Das Reich *Division pass through Rumania on their way to Yugoslavia in early 1941. It was soldiers of the division's motorcycle reconnaissance battalion who would capture the Yugoslav capital, Belgrade, in a daring episode, which succeeded because of bluff rather than military might.*

uled to begin on 15 May. A hostile Yugoslav government was a potential menace to both operations.

In early February 1941 the *Leibstandarte* was transferred to Rumania from France in preparation for 'Marita'. On 28 March an order to continue to Temesvar in southwestern Rumania was given to the *Verfügungs* Division, now renamed *Das Reich* Division. It was to leave its base at Versoul in eastern France and speed through Munich, Vienna and Budapest and on to the Rumanian-Yugoslavian frontier. The division's entire strength relocated in a feat of military logistics that took less than one week.

During the move, incidents occurred that resulted in serious hostility between Waffen-SS units and their army opposite numbers. In one instance, elements of a former Totenkopfstandarte, now SS-Infantry Regiment 11, were in a convoy of mixed units moving slowly east. An SS officer became inflamed by what he considered poor discipline when he saw that army vehicles were overtaking his floundering group. One army column was halted by the volatile and arrogant officer. Teller mines were placed under the front wheels of the leading vehicle, and an armed guard was placed with fixed bayonets to ensure they were not removed. The army troops were then informed no further movement would be permitted until the SS units had continued on their way. There were numerous incidents of

this nature serious enough to warrant a formal complaint from the Commander-in-Chief Field Marshal von Brauchitsch to Himmler.

Das Reich approaches Belgrade

Operation 'Marita' opened on 6 April 1941. As part of General Georg-Hans Reinhardt's XLI Panzer Corps, the *Reich* Division was involved in the thrust on Belgrade. The main road leading from Alibunar to Zagreb was the initial objective. General Reinhardt had promised to give movement priority as a prize to the first unit to reach the city, allowing it to take pole position in the assault on the capital. *Reich* had the mission of advancing over hostile terrain which comprised boggy marshland. It seemed to SS-Gruppenführer Paul 'Papa' Hausser that there would be little chance of his unit achieving this prize, but the divisional commander was undeterred.

The push for the Alibunar to Zagreb road by *Reich* began at 0900 hours on 11 April. The Yugoslav Army, weak and poorly equipped, was able to field only token resistance, so the Germans' main enemy was the weather, which turned the roads into muddy cart tracks, making rapid deployment all but impossible.

Reich had a Kradschutzen Battalion, or motorcycle reconnaissance battalion, which was able to ride along railway tracks. By this method, elements of the division were able to reach the road first. On the arrival of the rest of the division, orders were

Below: SS-Hauptsturmführer Fritz Klingenberg, the Das Reich *junior officer who captured Belgrade with a handful of men, recounts his story for the benefit of German radio listeners. Klingenberg went on to command the SS division* Götz von Berlichingen *before being killed in action in April 1945.*

received that all units were to halt at the River Danube. *Das Reich*'s initiative had seemingly been wasted.

SS-Hauptsturmführer Fritz Klingenberg and his motorcycle reconnaissance troops from 2 Company of the Kradschutzen were the first unit to reach the Danube on 11 April. Here Klingenberg found none of the bridges intact and the Danube so swollen that a crossing seemed impossible. Pressing into service a captured fishing boat, he managed to ferry himself and 10 volunteers from his command, with their motorcycles, onto the opposite side, whence this minuscule force set forth towards Belgrade.

They found the city virtually deserted apart from work gangs clearing up the rubble left by the Luftwaffe's bombing. They were practically ignored as they marched through the streets towards the German Embassy, and were setting up machine-gun posts when Klingenberg met the German military attaché, who had come to ask him to take the embassy staff under protection. An audacious plan formed in Klingenberg's mind, and together the two men set out to locate the mayor to persuade him to surrender the city. Klingenberg introduced himself to the unfortunate official as the commander of a major German

assault force that was at the gates of the city and issued an ultimatum: surrender or an air strike by the dreaded Stukas would be called down. The official believed him and Belgrade was handed over to Klingenberg and his men at 1845 hours. The advance guard of the 11th Panzer Division arrived during the night to find the surrender of the Yugoslav capital had been secured by a handful of Waffen-SS troops.

The 7th Armoured Division from Barcs was only a few hours behind, the Hungarians were in the plain beyond the Danube, and the vanguard of the German XLI Corps, which crossed into the Banat from Temesvar on Friday morning, was rapidly approaching the city. The following morning, Easter Day, the German authorities took over the capital. On 14 May, Klingenberg was decorated by Hitler with the Knight's Cross for his bold victory.

The taking of the Klidi Pass

The 12th Army, commanded by General Wilhelm List, was on the southern sector. It was composed of four panzer divisions, eight infantry divisions and the army's elite *Grossdeutschland* Regiment, together with the *Leibstandarte*. It was positioned to thrust into Greece at the start of the campaign on 6 April. The *Leibstandarte* Division attacked from Rumania, by way of Bulgaria and southern Yugoslavia, in conjunction with the 9th Panzer Division. Skopje was taken in the course of their advance and within three days they were at the stronghold of Monastir on the Yugoslav-Greek border, which they overcame. From the start of the campaign the *Leibstandarte* suffered only five wounded.

The Klidi Pass, the gateway to Greece, was defended by veteran Australians and New Zealanders of the British Expeditionary Force (BEF). On 10 April the *Leibstandarte* began the assault. The 1st Battalion was deployed as a mountain unit, climbing the rocky sides of the pass supported by fire from the

Left: The Waffen-SS rolls into Greece in April 1941. The Leibstandarte *Division fought superbly in Greece, and a number of its officers distinguished themselves, such as SS-Sturmbannführer Kurt Meyer, whose actions resulted in the SS capturing the strategically important Klissura Pass after bitter fighting.*

regiment's 88mm guns. While the SS infantry worked their way up through the rocks, assault guns were brought in along the road and the far end of the pass was reached early the following morning. In an attempt to force the Germans back, a counterattack was staged by British tanks. They were forced to withdraw when the 88mm guns were again brought into play. It took the *Leibstandarte* two days before the momentum of their attack overwhelmed the defenders.

The advance units of the *Leibstandarte* had covered so much ground in such a short space of time that their heavy artillery had yet to catch up with them. Another mountain engagement lay ahead: the storming of the heavily defended Klissura Pass. As daylight faded on 11 April the forward elements of the *Leibstandarte* were nearing the foothills leading to the pass. The first ridges were in German hands within 30 minutes. Meeting no serious obstacles, the German vehicles motored high into the mountains until they came to a bridge over a shallow ravine that had been blown up, forcing them to stop. The Greek defenders in the rocks above poured machine-gun fire and threw grenades onto the German column below. To add to the mayhem, mortar shells began to land. Advance or retreat was impossible as the Germans' vehicles could not turn on the narrow mountain roads. Respite was afforded with the onset of night, when SS engineers blasted rocks out of the mountain into the ravine and on top of the ruined bridge. A human chain was formed and boulders were passed by hand until the ravine was filled. Building on this foundation a narrow section of the ravine was made passable.

The Greeks had been ordered to hold the pass to protect the retreat of III Greek Corps from the Albanian front, where it had been

Left: Leibstandarte *infantry in the mountains of Greece in April 1941. Dietrich pushed his men relentlessly, never giving the Greeks or their British and Commonwealth allies time to reorganise defence lines. At Kastoria, for example, the appearance of his men resulted in 12,000 Greeks surrendering.*

behind the partially destroyed mountain road. The troops were reluctant to press on and Meyer, demonstrating the unorthodox leadership methods of the SS, lobbed a grenade behind his rearmost man. The SS then pushed forward towards the summit, finally extinguishing the last vestiges of resistance with the concentrated fire of machine-guns, 88s and grenades.

Meyer takes Kastoria

The *Leibstandarte*'s next objective was Koritza, the headquarters of III Greek Corps. It started its descent into the plain immediately. The approaches to Kastoria were being reconnoitred by that afternoon, when concentrated Greek artillery fire made it withdraw. The infantry alone could not easily take these positions so it was necessary to bring up the 3rd Battalion and call on the support of the *Leibstandarte*'s regimental artillery. A squadron of Stukas was also called in and a furious bombardment was unleashed on the Greeks. The SS infantry stormed into Greek positions that were overcome before their occupants had time to recover.

Armoured cars of Meyer's reconnaissance detachment approached the city of Kastoria at breakneck speed. Large columns of retreating Greek troops met on the way quickly surrendered. Kastoria was in German hands by late afternoon with over 11,000 Greek prisoners taken.

On 19 April the *Leibstandarte* was ordered to capture the Metsovan Pass. It pushed forwards against crumbling resistance and by

fighting the Italians. Its escape was imperative so it might join other Greek, British and Commonwealth troops in the defence of the southern part of the country. The defenders were well dug-in, with the advantage of supporting fire from their mountain artillery.

The assault fell to the *Leibstandarte*'s Aufklärungsabteilung, or reconnaissance battalion, commanded by SS-Sturmbannführer Kurt Meyer. Two companies clambered up the cliffs under cover of darkness

behind the Greek defenders and were ready to attack at first light. In the meantime an advance party of about 30 men led by Meyer began moving through the pass.

As Meyer's group advanced up the road, shells blew huge craters in it. The main demolition charges had been set off by the Greek defenders, and through the smoke and clouds of dirt machine-gun fire raked the pass, forcing Meyer and his men to take cover. The situation was critical: before them lay the enemy and

20 April the SS units had captured the pass, thus cutting through the withdrawal road of the Greek Epirus Army, isolating its 16 divisions west of the Pindus range and forcing their surrender on 21 April.

This left the BEF to fight on alone. On 24 April the *Leibstandarte* moved south towards Mesolongion and then east towards Navpaktos on the Gulf of Corinth, in pursuit of the retreating British and Commonwealth forces. The chase continued across the Gulf of Corinth and on through Peloponnesus. Behind a screen of gallant rearguards the British managed to evacuate most of their troops over the gulf to Patras. Meyer and his reconnaissance unit continued the pursuit, pressing into service every fishing boat that could be found to ferry his battalion across into Patras.

The following morning Meyer gave orders to his battalion's 2 Company to go east to Corinth and make contact with units of Paratroop Regiment 2. The SS troops had to commandeer whatever vehicles were available locally to do so and then returned to Patras to begin their march south towards Olympia in pursuit of the fleeing British. Owing to lack of fuel the British were forced to abandon their vehicles, which were quickly and gratefully appropriated by the SS. Before its advance was halted, the *Leibstandarte* reached as far south as Olympia. The Greek Army's collapse and the evacuation of the British and Commonwealth forces rendered any further advance unnecessary.

Right: 'Sepp' Dietrich during the Greek Campaign. He accepted the surrender of 16 Greek divisions on 21 April, which angered the Italian dictator Mussolini, who believed only he should receive such a reward. While Il Duce blustered, Dietrich continued the pursuit of retreating British and Commonwealth forces.

On 27 April German troops entered Athens, and three days later the Germans were in complete control of the country. Once again the *Leibstandarte* was accorded the honour of participating in the victory parade, this time held in Athens in front of Field Marshal List. The SS brigade was subsequently sent north to Prague to be refitted for its next offensive, Operation Barbarossa – the invasion of the Soviet Union.

Altogether the whirlwind Balkan campaign took some 223,000 Greek and 21,900 British prisoners. German losses for the entire campaign were 2559 dead, 5820 wounded and 3169 missing.

The high-profile achievements registered in the campaign by the *Leibstandarte SS Adolf Hitler* and *Das Reich* Divisions gave added credence, in the eyes of their Führer, to the standing of these élite troops. Hitler was now convinced that the Waffen-SS should be expanded, which led to the creation of two new Waffen-SS divisions: *Wiking* and *Nord*.

CHAPTER 5

CRUSADE IN THE EAST

The attack on Russia in June 1941 was, for the Waffen-SS, a crusade against Bolshevism, the Jews and 'subhumanity', in which the soldiers of Himmler's elite fought fanatically to prove the superiority of 'Nordic blood'. It was to be the beginning of four years of brutal warfare, in which the Waffen-SS surpassed all expectations.

Left: Waffen-SS troops halt in a Russian village during the early phase of Operation 'Barbarossa'. The Waffen-SS's task was the destruction of the 'power of Bolshevism and the Jews'.

Above: Soldiers of the Das Reich *Division carry out their last-minute checks before going into action against Red Army units. The division was part of Field Marshal Fedor von Bock's Army Group Centre, and was not committed to battle until 28 June, when it forced a river crossing between Citva and Dukova.*

Hitler had never disguised from his generals that he regarded the Nazi-Soviet Pact as a temporary rather than permanent feature of Germany's strategy. In November 1939, discussing this corrosive 'friendship', he advised his commanders that 'We can oppose Russia only when we are free in the West', assuring them that for the moment Russia 'is not dangerous'. In the summer of 1940 Hitler finally had his 'freedom' in the West, but with Britain refusing to surrender, his liberty of action, for all his rasping proclamation of conquest, seemed somewhat curtailed. War with the Soviet Union was a decision, the enormity of which was only equalled by its rapidity, a paradox, but one perhaps less baffling if viewed not as strategic or military rationality in the normal sense, but as Hitler's own brand of it. The temptation, the power, the occasion and the frustration born

out of the failure to knock out Britain 'at one blow' all combined to give this stupendous step a form and reality all its own. Years of brooding and moments of intoxication thus fused fiercely into what General Warlimont subsequently called 'this ghastly development'.

Führer Directive No. 21 was given on 18 December 1940, setting out the objectives of the campaign, planned to be launched in May the following year. This Directive stated:

'The bulk of the Russian army stationed in western Russia will be destroyed by daring operations led by deeply penetrating armoured spearheads. Russian forces still capable of giving battle will be prevented from withdrawing into the depths of Russia.

'The enemy will then be energetically pursued and a line will be reached from which the Russian air

Right: The Waffen-SS powers into Russia at the start of 'Barbarossa'. The nature of the struggle ahead was set down in Nazi Party orders: 'Obedience must be unconditional. It corresponds to the conviction that National Socialist ideology must reign supreme. Every SS man is therefore prepared to carry out blindly every order.'

force can no longer attack German territory. The final objective of the operation is to erect a barrier against Asiatic Russia on the general line Volga-Archangel. The last surviving industrial areas of Russia in the Urals can then, if necessary, be eliminated by the Luftwaffe.'

Hitler was now launched on his crusade like the standard bearer of his Directive 21 Emperor Frederic Barbarossa, one of the heroes of

German history who at the close of the 12th century marched with his knights against the infidel in the Holy Land. The campaign in Russia was to be a crusade based on a clash of ideologies, which could be perceived as quasi religious, National Socialism versus Communism. It was for the subjugation of those the Party despised most: the Jews, Slavs and Bolsheviks. The Herrenvolk or master race would be in Wagnerian struggle against the Untermenschen, or sub-humans. The Third Reich's ideological and military élite, the Waffen-SS, would encounter a new kind of war. The battles in the Soviet Union brought spectacular victories but also brutality of unimaginable magnitude, with both sides giving and receiving no quarter.

Stalin's purges struck the armed forces fearfully. They were named the 'Tukhachedsky purges' after Marshal Mikhail Tukhachedsky, the most prominent officer executed. Few events had more influence on the Soviet Red Army of 1941 than the systematic destruction of the Soviet High Command which Stalin carried out between 1937 and 1939. Heydrich had been helped by SS-Gruppenführer Dr Hermann Behrends and SS-Sturmbannführer Alfred Naujocks with the Tukhachedsky affair and the information

gained helped colour the timing and content of Directive 21. Heydrich boasted he had destroyed the Soviet High command. Primarily, Stalin's motive in purging the army was to secure his position as absolute ruler of the Soviet Union. Since the army possessed arms and in addition leaders who did not owe their positions, authority or prestige to Stalin those leaders must be destroyed, just as his party colleagues had been destroyed in 1936–37. Three out of five marshals of the Soviet Union, 11 deputy commissars of defence, 13 out of 15 army commanders and all the military district commanders of May 1937 as well as the leading members of the naval and air force commands were shot during this period or disappeared without trace. The political apparatus which

was supposed to advise the professional soldiers suffered the same fate. Altogether some 35,000 officers were dismissed, imprisoned or executed during those two fearful years, a purge which was to cause incalculable damage to the ability of the Soviet Red Army to resist the German invasion. Stalin's dreaded secret police, the NKVD, had achieved what the German military command and Heydrich's secret service could never have done.

The balance of forces

Eleven German armies, four of them panzer and three air fleets, totalling approximately three million soldiers accompanied by 3330 tanks and 2770 aircraft, were pitted against the Soviet Red Army, which was still operationally and logistically

paralysed by the loss of some of its brightest and ablest men. However, the odds appears at first sight to be uneven, with the Soviet Red Army comprising 230 divisions totalling some twelve million men supported by 20,000 tanks and 8000 aircraft. Yet only about 130 were deployed in the path of the Wehrmacht.

The Waffen-SS units were deployed among the Army commands. Army Group South, which comprised five Panzer, three to four

Below: Members of the Das Reich *Division pause on the edge of a wood near Yelna in late July 1941. The town was the location of an important road junction, and was taken by the* Deutschland *and* Der Führer *Regiments of the division, assisted by tanks from the 10th Panzer Division, after heavy fighting against the Russians.*

motorised, 21–22 infantry, six mountain and three security divisions conjoined with 14–15 Rumanian, two Hungarian and two Italian divisions under the command of Field Marshal Gerd von Rundstedt, was allocated the *Leibstandarte SS Adolf Hitler* and *Wiking* divisions, which were with General Edwald von Kleist's 1st Panzer Group.

Das Reich was allocated to Guderian's 2nd Panzer Group, part of Army Group Centre which comprised nine Panzer, five motorised and 31–35 infantry divisions as well as two to three security divisions, a cavalry division and the *Grossdeutschland* Regiment under Field Marshal Fedor von Bock.

Army Group North, the weakest of the Army Groups with only three Panzer, three motorised and about 20 infantry divisions, commanded by Field Marshal Ritter von Leeb, had the *Totenkopf* Division assigned to it as part of General Erich Höppner's 4th Panzer Group. The *Polizei* Division was part of Army Group North's reserves, while Battle group *Nord* and SS Infantry Regiment 9 were deployed as part of the Norway Mountain Corps under the command of Colonel General von Falkenhorst and committed to the far northern sector of the front in Finland.

The grand plan

The initial task to cut off all the Soviet armies west of the Dnieper was allocated to Army Group South. The territorial objectives were to capture Kiev, Kharkov and the Crimea before pushing on to the River Volga where stood Stalingrad, a city of huge psychological importance. Next were the vital Caucasian oil fields. This force of some 46 divisions, comprising the 6th, 11th and 17th Armies and 1st Panzer Group, was to drive east in what was an over-ambitious plan. The *Leibstandarte* was assigned to XIV corps

of 1st Panzer Group. The Russian lines south of Kowel were the objective of 1st Panzer Group, which was to break through and cut off Soviet Red Army units to the southwest, containing them until such time as they were eliminated by the infantry. An advance over 480km (143 miles) had to be undertaken across difficult terrain with few Russian roads being metal-surfaced. Speed was of the essence, for once rains started, the dirt roads would be transformed into quagmires.

Above: A motorcycle patrol of the Leibstandarte *Division moves through a burning Russian town during Operation 'Barbarossa'. Near Klevan soldiers of the division found some mutilated corpses of their comrades. Divisional orders were immediately issued that the Russians 'must be slaughtered ruthlessly'.*

Making full use of the natural obstacles of the Rivers Pruth, San, Bug and Dnieper, the Russians deployed their lines of defences. Here the Soviet Red Army, under the

command of General Kirponos and then Marshal Budyenni, had a force of approximately 69 infantry, 11 cavalry and 28 armoured divisions opposing Army Group South

Operation 'Barbarossa', which was to be hailed as the greatest continuous land battle history had ever witnessed, opened on the morning of 22 June 1941 at 0315 hours. The pale dawn was seared by the sudden flashes of thousands of guns that heralded the clash of Titans. The Wehrmacht was about to inflict havoc upon the Soviet Red Army. All the Waffen-SS formations under Army command were in action within the first few days of the campaign, with the exception of the *Polizei* Division, which by early August was also engaged. Two brigades of Himmler's Kommandostab RFSS, SS Infantry Brigade 1 and SS Cavalry Brigade were deployed immediately behind the front operating against Russian troops bypassed during the main advance.

The *Leibstandarte* enters the fray

On 27 June the *Leibstandarte* left its assembly area and joined the reserve of 1st Panzer Group, where it was committed to battle. But it was not until 1 July, at a point southwest of the town of Zamosc, where it crossed the River Vistula, that it finally went into combat. The two arms of 1st Panzer Group's pincer movement were well extended by this time into Soviet territory and General von Mackensen's III Panzer Corps had been cut off near Rovno. Re-establishing contact with von Mackesen's corps was the first major task of the eastern campaign assigned to the *Leibstandarte*.

Soviet tanks were soon engaged by German forward elements. A German column, while pushing

Above: The city of Zhitomir, which was captured by the Leibstandarte *Division in July 1941. At the beginning of the month the Russians launched a series of desperate counterattacks against the invading Germans along the entire southwestern front. The fighting was often hand-to-hand and always vicious.*

through a densely wooded area, had two Soviet tanks attach themselves to it in the misconception that it was a retreating Soviet unit. Just outside Klevan as night was falling the column came to a brief halt. Here the awful truth was realised by the Soviet tank crews, who broke away from the column and sped off into the darkness.

The advance continued after Klevan had been quickly taken, then, a few kilometres to the east of the town, lead elements of the *Leibstandarte*'s reconnaissance battalion reached a spot where an

Right: During the first few weeks of Operation 'Barbarossa' the Germans achieved incredible gains along the whole front in Russia. Alongside the military effort ran the ideological campaign, which included the infamous 'Commissar Order', which commanded that Red Army political commissars be executed.

empty, blood-soaked ambulance was discovered beside an abandoned German howitzer. The SS troops fanned out and discovered the corpses of several German soldiers lying a few hundred metres away. Their bodies were mutilated and barbed wire bound their hands. The Waffen-SS replied to the atrocity in like manner, pronouncing that the Russians 'must be slaughtered ruthlessly'.

III Panzer Corps found that the armoured units which were attached to it were making such rapid progress that they were causing great gaps to open up between the widely dispersed German formations. These gaps were spotted by the Soviets, who attempted to exploit them, attacking out of the Pripet Marshes to the north. The so-called Rollbahn Nord, the main German supply route, was the Soviet primary target. If this could be cut it would deny supplies of ammunition, food and fuel to the advancing and vastly extended German units. The 1st Panzer Group, heading towards Zhitomir and Kiev, was to be given flanking cover by the *Leibstandarte*, which soon found itself fending off frenzied attacks by Soviet forces, which were often supported by armour.

At Mirupol, the Stalin Line defences were breached on 7 July by spearhead units of the *Leibstandarte*. They then pushed east towards Zhitomir, encountering stiff Soviet resistance. The Germans were often obliged to strike out across country as many roads were rendered impassable due to the

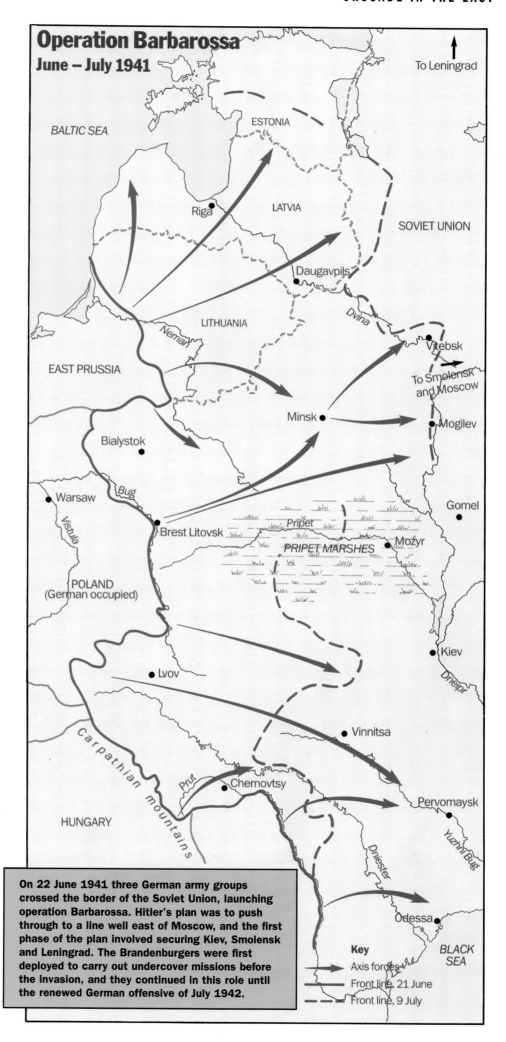

Operation Barbarossa
June – July 1941

To Leningrad

BALTIC SEA

ESTONIA

Riga · LATVIA

SOVIET UNION

Daugavpils

LITHUANIA

Dvina

Neman

Vitebsk

EAST PRUSSIA

To Smolensk and Moscow

Bialystok

Minsk · Mogilev

Warsaw · Bug

Pripet

Gomel

Vistula

Brest Litovsk

PRIPET MARSHES

Mozyr

POLAND
(German occupied)

Kiev

Dnepr

Lvov

Carpathian mountains

Vinnitsa

Prut

Chernovtsy

Pervomaysk

HUNGARY

Dniester

Yuzhni Bug

Odessa

Key

Axis forces

Front line, 21 June

Front line, 9 July

BLACK SEA

On 22 June 1941 three German army groups crossed the border of the Soviet Union, launching operation Barbarossa. Hitler's plan was to push through to a line well east of Moscow, and the first phase of the plan involved securing Kiev, Smolensk and Leningrad. The Brandenburgers were first deployed to carry out undercover missions before the invasion, and they continued in this role until the renewed German offensive of July 1942.

heavy rains that lashed the country. As nightfall fell at Romanovka, the spearhead units had been joined by the majority of the *Leibstandarte*.

The situation at the front was so fluid at this time that it was not only Soviet units that strayed. How far ahead of their parent units the reconnaissance elements could penetrate is shown by one incident in particular. SS-Obersturmbannführer Kurt Meyer, who had already distinguished himself and his unit in Greece, had left the main body of his battalion behind when he discovered that his small group had unwittingly passed through a gap between two Soviet units. Their infantry quickly surrounded Meyer and his troops, then an officer stepped towards him. Meyer's salute was returned and the two men shook hands. The Soviet officer was offered a cigarette, which he gratefully accepted. The Soviets were under the illusion that Meyer and his group wished to surrender. Meyer

perceived the confusion and in his inimitable manner demanded, via his interpreter, that it was indeed the Soviets who should surrender. Walking among the Soviet soldiers, he indicated that they should lay down their weapons and at the same time passed out cigarettes among them. The Soviet officer was neither impressed nor taken in by Meyer's theatricals. The ever-perceptive Meyer asked his interpreter quietly to play for time, as he hoped and expected at any moment that other elements of the battalion would be arriving. The argument about exactly who should surrender to whom continued, with the Soviet officer becoming irritated. It seemed Meyer's bluff had failed when into view came a German armoured car, which was promptly hit by a Soviet anti-tank shell. Another armoured car appeared and returned the fire. At this point Meyer screamed to his troops to let loose with everything and a furious fire-

Above: Operation 'Barbarossa' brought spectacular gains for the Wehrmacht's panzers. Army Group Centre, for example, in the first month of the campaign, had inflicted losses on the enemy on a scale never contemplated before in war. By 15 July it was almost 800km (500 miles) to the east of its start point.

fight developed. The balance was shifted in Meyer's favour with the arrival of German armour and the Soviets were neutralised.

Storming across the Teterev

Just west of Zhitomir stood the vital Keednov road junction, which was captured by the *Leibstandarte* on 8 July in a battle fought principally by Meyer's battalion. Supported by 88mm artillery fire, his reconnaissance troops stormed across the River Teterev.

On some occasions at least the Soviets were proving to be more worthy opponents than the Germans had given them credit for.

Gaps in the German lines were continually forming between the fast-moving armoured units in the spearheads and the slower-moving infantry divisions following behind. These the Soviets were masterful at exploiting.

Army Group South had in essence achieved its primary objective and the bulk of the Soviet armies in the southwest been destroyed. This was the feeling of the OKW, the high command of the German armed forces, but the troops at the front did not share this optimism. A Soviet counteroffensive began, contradicting this over-optimistic viewpoint. The Soviet thrust once again

Right: An image which typifies Operation 'Barbarossa': panzers racing past burning Russian towns and villages. For the Waffen-SS the campaign in Russia was the fulfilment of a dream. This dream, in Himmler's words, 'an ideological battle and a struggle of races', turned into a nightmare for the Russian population.

had the objective of cutting the main supply route. This was to prove by no means an easy task but finally the Soviet attacks were beaten off, often by ferocious hand-to-hand fighting in which knives, bayonets and entrenching tools were employed. Much of the fighting raged through wooded areas and casualties were heavy on both sides. The terrain gave rise to its own form of hell, lethal wood splinters showering the combatants as shells burst in the trees. Because of the fluidity of the battle lines, neither side knew exactly who was out-manoeuvring whom or who was gaining the upper hand. On 9 July Shepkova was captured by the *Leibstandarte* when the enemy pressure was temporarily eased, allowing it to go onto the offensive.

The attack in the south, an advance in the direction of Kiev, was unexpectedly altered to a drive towards Uman by Hitler on 10 July.

Left: French volunteers in the Wehrmacht during the invasion of Russia. For the Waffen-SS, the attack on Russia provided a boost to the recruitment of foreigners into the Waffen-SS. A few days after the start of the invasion, Hitler approved the formation of national legions to be raised in western Europe to fight in Russia.

General Kempf gave special praise for the contribution made by the *Leibstandarte* in the Uman Pocket: 'The *Leibstandarte SS Adolf Hitler* has played a most glorious part in the encirclement of enemy forces around Uman. Committed at the height of the battle for the seizure of the enemy positions at Archangelsk, it took the city and the high ground to the south with incomparable dash. In a spirit of devoted brotherhood of arms, the *Leibstandarte SS Adolf Hitler* intervened on its own initiative in the desperate situation which had developed for 16th Infantry Division on its left flank, routing the enemy and destroying many tanks. Today, with the battle of annihilation around Uman concluded, I wish to recognise, and express my special gratitude to the *Leibstandarte SS Adolf Hitler* for their exemplary efforts and incomparable bravery.'

On 29 June 1941, led by the *Westland* Regiment, the *Wiking* Division moved forward decisively from its start point on the northern wing of Army Group South and

Below: The mood is relaxed and jovial as the Wehrmacht and its allies continue to advance into Russia. The weather is still warm and the Russians are retreating. But despite the victories, such as the one at Smolensk which netted 750,000 prisoners, the Red Army showed no signs of giving up the struggle.

The objective of the alteration in thrust was to cut off the Soviet armies there and surround them. This resulted in this sector experiencing weeks of savage fighting. XXXVIII Corps had the *Leibstandarte* allocated to it, and on 31 July was ordered to push against Novo Archangelsk to close the Uman Pocket. This area saw the Soviets throw their whole weight into battle in their attempts to break out of the German encirclement. These attacks sometimes comprised massed Soviet infantry formations supported by concentrated armour, the combined strength of which made them difficult to hold off. The Nebelwerfer, a multi-barrelled rocket launcher which made a groaning howl as it fired, was put to good use by the SS troops and the SS lines held firm, with the result that the Soviet breakthrough attempts ultimately weakened. When the Uman Pocket surrendered over 100,000 men were captured from the Soviet 6th and 12th Armies.

advanced through Soviet-occupied Poland. On 30 June Lemberg was reached by spearhead units, which ran into the Soviet 32nd Infantry Division. The Soviet forces, which were numerically superior, put considerable pressure on the Waffen-SS elements, which had to withstand repeated attempts to push them back. Finally the balance swung in the German favour with the arrival of armour from the division's reconnaissance battalion and the Soviet counterattacks were able to be repulsed. During this action SS-Standartenführer Hilmar Wackerle, the commander of the *Westland* Regiment, while driving in his command car was fatally wounded by a single shot fired by a lone Soviet straggler. This was a great loss to the regiment.

Wiking at the Stalin Line

A crossing of the River Slucz at Husyantin was forced by the Waffen-SS troops, and lead units from *Wiking* Division were soon in the thick of the fighting once more. This formed part of the Stalin Line defences, where they encountered particularly strong Soviet forces, which counterattacked immediately. Things began to look bleak for the Germans for some time as the fighting raged back and forth until the arrival on the scene of the army's 1st Mountain Division, which relieved the beleaguered force,

Driving towards Kozmin on 8 July, *Wiking* Division became engulfed in a torrential downpour, which turned the mud roads into a quagmire and reduced the division's speed to snail's pace, and that only achieved with great difficulty. The divisional HQ at Toratscha was nearly overrun, and there was bitter fighting that involved the *Germania* and *Nordland* regiments. Continuing its push eastwards on foot, the *Westland* Regiment went on a four-day forced march through heavily wooded

terrain to the River Ross. Abandoned Soviet material and vehicles were littered all around in vast quantities ,and by 23 July *Wiking* Division was picking its way through these masses of debris. At this point III Panzer Corps temporarily took control of the division, while to assist in the battles around Uman, the *Westland* Regiment was diverted at speed south to Talnoze.

Fighting to secure the northern flank of 1st Panzer Group around Korsun and Schandorovka, elements from *Wiking* Division served alongside the Luftwaffe's élite *Hermann Göring* Regiment from

Above: A German flamethrower deals with a Russian strongpoint near Kiev in September 1941. The Das Reich *Division participated in the encirclement of the city, which fell on 26 September. The Germans captured 665,000 prisoners, 884 tanks and 3718 guns – no less than five Russian armies had been destroyed.*

7 to 16 August. To help contain Soviet attacks, a battle group from the *Westland* Regiment was also despatched to Dnepropetrovsk.

When the Uman Pocket surrendered, 1st Panzer Group moved in the direction of Bobry, renewing its advance. On 9 August the town

street and every house. Heavy casualties on both sides were incurred due to the bitter house-to-house fighting. The degree of fanaticism shown in the defence off their homeland by some of the Soviet units was becoming apparent to the Germans as their casualties mounted; the qualities of fearlessness and determination demonstrated by Soviet troops in hand-to-hand combat were equal to those possessed by the Waffen-SS, and cost the Germans dear. The *Leibstandarte* finally took the city on 20 August, after three days of fierce fighting. A few precious days of rest and reorganisation was bestowed upon the division as a reward, then the Dnieper was crossed and the division struck out once again across the barren steppe.

Victory on the Dnieper

To the north, a small bridgehead over the Dnieper at Dnepropetrovsk had been established by German units. This area had been the home of a Soviet artillery school whose artillery cadets had expertly plotted the entire district, with the result that the Soviets had little difficulty in pinpointing German targets, which came under heavy Soviet artillery fire. *Nordland*, *Westland* and *Germania* crossed the river at the bridgehead, then the former pushed north towards Mogila Ostraya, while the latter two reinforced the units on the bridgehead's western edge and on 6–7 September captured the heights at Kamenka, collecting over 5000 Soviet prisoners.

Once again, in an attempt to exploit the gaps between the German units, the Soviets mounted a surprise counterattack which saw German-held territory penetrated to a depth of 32km (20 miles) by the Soviet forces. In the hope of eliminating this new Soviet threat the *Leibstandarte* was hastily brought back over the Dnieper. On

fell, the Soviet defence, consisting in the main of cavalry units, being soon overrun. The *Leibstandarte* then moved on to Zaselye, which was quickly taken. No sooner had it fallen than a furious counterattack was mounted by the Soviets. Grimly holding on to its positions, the *Leibstandarte* struggled for a whole week against the Soviets, who with equal determination tried to force it out. The attacks finally came to an end on 17 August, with Russian losses totalling approximately 1000 men taken prisoner, killed or wounded.

Above: Street fighting in Kiev in September 1941. During the encirclement of the city the Das Reich *Division had seized a vital bridge over the River Desna. The bridge had been wired for demolition by the Russians, but the sheer speed of the Waffen-SS attack had taken the defenders totally by surprise.*

Cherson, a large city in an industrial area, was the next objective for the *Leibstandarte*. The Waffen-SS infantry, for the first time in Russia, would be forced to storm a sizeable city. The Soviet naval infantry who defended Cherson contested every

9 September, the Germans took Novya Mayatschka, and within a couple of days Novo Alexandrovka was passed by the *Leibstandarte* on its drive east.

Hitler once again changed his plans. Soviet troops had been withdrawing into the Crimea in large numbers. A narrow neck of land, which had been heavily fortified and was well-defended, provided the only access. Hitler decided that rather than simply bypass the Crimea, this potential threat to the flank of the German advance had to be eradicated.

The Perkop Isthmus, the entrance to the Crimea, was where the *Leibstandarte* made its first attempt to force its way through on the western side. Here its path was blocked by deep minefields, well-prepared fortifications and the added problem of armoured trains, which were heavily armed. The eastern edge of the Crimean 'neck' was the division's next assault point as the Perkop Isthmus defences proved far too strong to be penetrated. There, in a dawn attack under cover of dense fog, the enemy defences were penetrated and the division stormed

past Balykov to capture high ground at Genichek. From their vantage point the Waffen-SS troops could observe the Soviets undergoing preparations for a counterattack, which allowed them to implement their defence strategy accordingly.

The *Leibstandarte* in the Crimea

Once the entrance to the Crimea had been secured by the *Leibstandarte* Division it continued pushing eastwards on the Russian 'mainland' in the direction of Melitopol, and on 18 September reached Rodianovka, where it dug in. The German positions were the objects of several counterattacks which were rebuffed successfully before the Waffen-SS troops were moved westwards, once again to another crisis spot.

While the Crimea was being attacked by LIV corps, the Romanian troops holding a sector of the German lines were subjected to vicious counterattacks by Soviet units which smashed deep into it, virtually annihilating them. The Waffen-SS were once again in demand, and the mainstay of the German defence was the elite

troops of the *Leibstandarte*. The steam had run out of the Soviet attacks by 30 September. Once more 1st Panzer Group could continue advancing eastwards, with Rostov on the River Don now in its sights.

On 11 October Taganrog was reached by the *Leibstandarte*, which had aggressively driven eastwards over inhospitable terrain for almost 400km (248 miles). The River Mius had to be crossed before the assault on the city could begin and this was achieved under heavy fire. Taganrog was taken after six days, during which time the fighting had raged continuously, and Stalino fell three days later.

III Panzer Corps lost *Wiking* Division on 10 October, when it was transferred to XIV Panzer Corps. Its objective was to overtake fleeing Soviet units and cut them off. In an

Below: German troops flush out defenders in yet another Russian town. As they pushed deeper into the Soviet Union, the Germans found that resistance stiffened. When the Leibstandarte *Division assaulted the industrial city of Cherson in August 1941, for example, it took three days of house-to-house fighting to win it.*

attempt to achieve this it advanced along the Melitopol to Stalino railway line towards Wolnowacha. Once again the roads were turned into seas of mud by torrential rain, with the result that progress was slowed dramatically. The Russians now had time to reassemble their scattered units and regroup, as the rain fell continuously for more than a fortnight.

The *Westland* Regiment received a new form of baptism of fire at the beginning of November, when it was subjected to a barrage from Katyushas for the first time. The psychological effect on the Waffen-

Below: One of the Wehrmacht's much-vaunted panzers in Russia (this is a Panzer IV). As the invasion of the Soviet Union continued, however, the panzers began encountering increasing numbers of the T-34 tank, which was fast, well armoured and had a 76mm gun. It could hold its own against any German tank.

SS troops was shattering. A salvo of these projectiles landing among unprepared and unprotected infantry units caused near panic.

With the onset of colder weather, the German units were able to achieve a much better degree of mobility for a few weeks as the muddy roads began to firm up once again. This was to change, however, when winter proper set in.

The attack on Rostov

The assault on Rostov began during mid-November, when the spearhead units had been reached by the bulk of III Panzer Corps. This essential communications link capture was greatly aided by the taking of a vital bridge over the River Don by SS-Hauptsturmführer Springer of the *Leibstandarte* Division on 20 November in a daring attack, for which he was awarded the Knight's Cross of the Iron Cross.

The rail bridge was still intact, although demolition charges had been set. It appeared that Soviet engineers were considering its imminent destruction. A locomotive, its boiler apparently with a full head of steam, was spotted waiting by the bridge. Springer ordered his men to open fire with every weapon available, resulting in the locomotive being peppered so that high-pressure steam issued from countless holes. The bridge was stormed under cover of the confusion and Springer and his men were able to remove the demolition charges. Although the Soviets made frenzied attempts to dislodge the Waffen-SS troops, they succeeded in holding

Right: 'Kick in the door,' Hitler had remarked to his generals concerning the attack on Russia, 'and the whole rotten superstructure will come crashing down.' But the door had been kicked in at Rostov, Kiev and Smolensk and still the Russians showed no signs of giving up. And the weather was starting to deteriorate.

Above: A motorcycle team of the Totenkopf *Division on the road to Leningrad. By October 1941 Eicke's men had suffered almost 9000 casualties since the beginning of the campaign (it had started with a strength of 18,754). Such attrition took a toll on the rate of advance, which further slowed with the onset of poor weather.*

the bridge until reinforcements arrived. Later the same day Rostov fell, and another 10,000 Russian prisoners were taken.

The scorching heat and choking dust of the Russian summer and the rains which produced quagmires everywhere, making roads into impassable rivers of mud, were the problems the Germans had experienced up to this stage. But the worst horror of all was about to face them: the Russian winter. The Germans were caught totally unprepared as temperatures began to plummet. They still wore the same summer uniforms they had been issued with at the beginning of the campaign in June and no warm winter clothing

was forthcoming. The German vehicles had the oil begin to freeze in their engines and sumps, while the mechanisms of the guns also froze. Worse still, if moisture formed in the barrels of the machine guns turned to ice, the gun split its barrel when it was fired again. To thaw out the engines of the vehicles enough to start them, the Germans had to light small fires under them.

The problems of winter were no hardship of course for the Soviet troops, who had fur-lined winter clothing in abundance. Russian weather conditions determined to a great extent the design of Soviet vehicles, which would still function when the cold rendered German vehicles useless.

The *Leibstandarte* had to retrace its steps westward into positions along the Mius river when the German position in Rostov became untenable and it was obliged to withdraw from the city. Because of the severity of the weather that followed soon afterwards, military operations of any significance throughout this whole sector were curtailed.

The praise and admiration of numerous senior army commanders had been earned by the *Leibstandarte* during this first phase of the war on the Eastern Front for both the offensive and defensive actions it had been involved in. Reichsführer-SS Heinrich Himmler was to receive an unsolicited letter from General von Mackensen in which he commented that in his opinion the *Leibstandarte* was 'a real elite unit'.

Schachty, a new objective further to the north, had been given to the *Wiking* Division to be taken before winter finally closed in. On 5 November, *Wiking*'s advance began, but once again the roads were turned into swamps as a result of a brief and unexpected thaw. The

Mius river was crossed and, in order to reach the road to Astoahowo, the Waffen-SS troops struggled towards the higher ground in the direction of Perwomaisk-Oktjabrisk. Instead of trucks carrying the troops, the conditions became so bad that the troops were obliged to disembark and push the trucks through the thick mud.

Wiking encounters stiff resistance

The German forces had become dangerously overstretched in an area between 16th and 14th Panzer Divisions. When the division reached Oktjabrisk on 7 November, a battle group was diverted south into it. During this period the German positions were continually being probed by Soviet units seeking weak spots; as a result *Germania* seemed in almost constant combat, while the Waffen-SS

troops attempted doggedly to push their advance forward. In the meantime, *Nordland* continued northeast with its thrust towards Alexandrovka.

The Germans were encountering a hardening of Soviet resistance. The Soviet T-34 tanks were being deployed in ever-increasing numbers, coming as a nasty shock not only to the German tank crews, but also to the anti-tank gunners. Up until then, anything in their path had been swept aside as they encountered mainly obsolete light, thinly

Below: One thing that struck the German soldiers who fought on the Eastern Front was the vast distances involved. The seemingly endless terrain seem to swallow up entire armies. The realisation began to dawn that it would take much more than a Blitzkrieg campaign lasting a few weeks to defeat the Russians.

armoured vehicles such as the BT-5 during the opening phase of the campaign. The T-34 was fast, reliable and well armoured, an animal to be feared, and into the bargain its 76mm gun delivered a decisive punch. Unless they were used at extremely close range, the 37mm anti-tank guns most German units were equipped with in 1941 were ineffective against them.

On 23 November XIV Panzer Corps was subjected to a counter-attack by powerful Soviet forces and was forced onto the defensive. The SS infantry were without adequate winter clothing and temperatures hit -20°C (-4°F). Conditions generally were worsening and many of them were soon crippled by frost-bite. The SS were gradually pushed back to defensive positions on the Tusloff river by the Soviet 9th and 37th Armies. Owing to lack of numbers of SS troops to defend the line of the river, which stretched a long way because of its many loops and curves, it became clear that it would be almost impossible to hold these positions, so the Germans were forced again to withdraw, this time to the River Mius further west. Here, around Amwrosjewka, they dug in.

Totenkopf dispositions

At the start of the campaign the *Totenkopf* Division was under the control of Army Group North, which was commanded by Field Marshal Wilhelm Ritter von Leeb. It

Above: What was all the death and destruction for? In Nazi Party language the Russian war involved 'the elimination of all racially and biologically inferior elements and the radical removal of all incorrigible political opposition that refuses on principle to acknowledge the ideological basis of National Socialism'.

comprised on the left the 18th Army commanded by General Kuchler, whose objective was to push east through Latvia and Estonia. In the centre the 4th Panzer Group was commanded by General Erich Höppner, who was to drive towards Leningrad. On the right, the 16th Army commanded by General Busch was tasked with giving flank protection.

overcome. The initial resistance that Höppner's troops encountered was extremely light, and on the first day alone they were able to cover 80 km (50 miles). Nearly 320 km (199 miles) into Soviet-held territory lay Dvinsk, which had been reached by 4th Panzer Group on 26 June and the bridges over the Dvina captured. Outpacing the slower moving infantry divisions, the spearhead units were obliged to halt at Dvinsk so that they might catch up.

The *Totenkopf* in the north

The southern flank of General von Manstein's LVI Panzer Corps and the northern flank of the 16th Army, its neighbour, had developed a considerable gap between them. Soviet stragglers in considerable numbers were still active behind the German armies, having been cut off as a result of the phenomenal rate of advance the Germans had achieved. To clear up these stragglers the *Totenkopf* Division was sent into action, during which time it moved up to Dvinsk to join the main force of the group. Soviet units, at first bewildered, began to reorganise and re-form after they recovered from

the initial shock of the German attack, and as the *Totenkopf* Division progressed it found resistance stiffening.

Moving through central Lithuania, the *Totenkopf* Division met more determined resistance on 27 June. The Division's reconnaissance battalion, its spearhead unit, was halted in its tracks when it ran into a sizeable enemy force with tank support. Eventually the tanks were repulsed but Soviet infantry attacks continued, mounted by fanatical, almost suicidal soldiers. Nevertheless, the *Totenkopf* Division troops still tried to maintain the pace of their advance, although their progress was significantly slowed as they fought back.

To assist in repelling the Soviet counterattacks on LVI Panzer Corps at Dvinsk it was decided to send

Below: The drive on Moscow continues. The armoured vehicle in the foreground is a StuG III self-propelled gun. Over 8000 StuG IIIs were manufactured and used in the war. They were issued to Waffen-SS panzergrenadier formations, often instead of tanks. Fortunately the StuG III was an excellent armoured fighting vehicle.

Höppner's 4th Panzer Group's principal units were XXXXI and LVI Panzer Corps, with the 269th Infantry Division and the *Totenkopf* Division in reserve. To keep the *Totenkopf* Division in reserve was a personal decision taken by Höppner, who had a dislike of Eicke together with his division – a decision that was highly unpopular with Eicke.

The Soviet border positions were smashed through by 4th Panzer Group on 22 June, the River Dvina and the key bridges that spanned it being its first objective.

An excellent natural obstacle was formed by the river, which ran from Vitebsk to the Gulf of Riga, and this the Germans would have to

Left: The strain begins to show on the face of this Waffen-SS soldier during a pause in the fighting. The rate of advance of the three German army groups led Hitler to believe that the 'Battle of Russia' had been completed within the first four weeks and all that remained was mopping up. The men at the front told a different story.

forced back under the weight of frenzied Soviet attacks. The timely appearance of Luftwaffe Stuka dive-bombers the following day relieved the situation, when they devastated the enemy artillery and tanks, allowing the initiative to be regained slowly by the *Totenkopf* Division. The advance got underway again and the *Totenkopf* Division captured Rosenov on 4 July.

Theodor Eicke is wounded

The *Totenkopf* Division smashed into the Stalin Line on 6 July and in its sector it found the defensive network particularly extensive. As a result the division took heavy losses but forced its way through, establishing a bridgehead over the River Velikaya by nightfall. Fierce artillery fire rained down on the soldiers of the *Totenkopf* Division and Eicke's command car hit a mine, leaving him wounded.

As part of the group reserve, the *Totenkopf* Division moved on 12 July to Porkhov. A few days of welcome rest was all that was forthcoming, as it was back in action on 17 July in support of LVI Panzer Corps, which had encountered trouble to the northeast of Porkhov. The LVI Panzer Corps' flanks had once again come under attack from the Soviet forces and the *Totenkopf* Division was sent to fend them off. The LVI Panzer Corps retained the *Totenkopf* Division with it, relieving the 8th Panzer Division, which went into reserve.

To the west of Lake Ilmen the *Totenkopf* Division once again began its advance on 21 July, moving

with all haste the Panzerjäger, or tank-hunter battalion, accompanied by one infantry battalion, while the remainder of the division followed. The *Totenkopf* Division became part of von Manstein's LVI Panzer Corps on reaching Dvinsk. It was joined here shortly afterwards by XXXXI Panzer Corps, followed by elements of the 16th Army.

Protecting Manstein's flank and maintaining contact with the 16th army was the *Totenkopf* Division's next assignment, to prevent dangerous gaps opening in the German line. Thus prepared, 4th Panzer

Group resumed its advance on 2 July. The terrain was ideal for straggling Soviet units to defend, being heavily wooded marshland. The *Totenkopf* Division now moved through this, finding it extremely difficult for a motorised unit to traverse. It was caught in a well-prepared ambush at Dagda by the Soviet 42nd Rifle Division, during which over 100 Waffen-SS troops were killed or wounded. The whole division was brought to a grinding halt by the sudden arrival of Soviet reinforcements, supported by armoured units, and it began to be

through the dark forests and swamps of the region. The Soviets had withdrawn to new defence lines, which ran along the Mshaga and Luga rivers, known as the Luga Line. A period that was to sap the strength and morale of the division then began on 8 August, when the *Totenkopf* began its assault on these positions. As soon as night fell the Soviets would initiate counter-attacks, utilising the cover of darkness. The *Totenkopf* Division troops then had to use all of their efforts during the day to force the determined defenders back. Rest was well-nigh impossible in any form. The Germans were enduring a battle of attrition, weakening their considerable strength, with fresh replacements taking time to acquire, while Soviet losses could apparently be made good without delay. The *Totenkopf* Division's rear areas had been infiltrated by partisans who were already operating behind the German lines. In addition, they had

managed to tap into the field telephone lines. From intercepted conversations they were able to glean where the *Totenkopf* Division's weak points were and plan their strategy of attacks accordingly. Another disaster to befall the *Totenkopf* Division troops occurred when they were hit by friendly fire, being strafed in error by Luftwaffe aircraft.

A handsome haul

A counterattack force was formed by amalgamating the *Totenkopf* Division and 3rd Motorised Division in mid-August to fight off the Soviet 34th Army, which was smashing into the German flanks. The two German divisions surreptitiously worked their way around to the flank and in turn crashed into the unsuspecting Soviets, with devastating effect. The 34th Army's shattered remnants were rounded up, and massive amounts of equipment as well as huge numbers of vehicles and

numerous Soviet prisoners were taken, with over 1000 prisoners being snatched by the *Totenkopf* Division's military police troop alone. Although this was an important victory for the Germans, with eight Soviet divisions destroyed, the attacking German units were significantly weakened as their losses were heavy.

On 22 August the advance resumed as the *Totenkopf* Division crossed the Polist and pushed eastwards towards the rivers Lovat and Pola. For several days the drive continued almost unhindered, with POWs being rounded up in considerable numbers. However, this

Below: A column of Waffen-SS trucks in Russia in late September 1941. The autumn rains are turning the roads into mud; more rain would reduce them to little more than swamps. This made effective military operations difficult, and also meant supply trucks had difficulty in getting to frontline units.

situation was not to last as the retreating Soviets had dug in and were waiting for the *Totenkopf* Division to reach the Lovat. The Luftwaffe had switched its efforts temporarily to other areas, giving the Soviets the advantage of considerable air support. Attempts to force a crossing of the river by the *Totenkopf* Division failed. The Soviet counterattacks were so powerful that the shelter provided by the woods near the river had to be sought by the Germans, who were then forced to withdraw further from the pursuing enemy forces (the Germans also had to avoid marauding Soviet fighters).

The renewal of *Totenkopf* Division's attack was ordered on 26 August with the objective of ousting the Soviets from their well-prepared positions, but once again the the division suffered considerable casualties in its endeavours – in fact the highest recorded casualty rate in the corps at this particular time. However, the skies over the Lovat once again became the Luftwaffe's domain on 27 August and it swiftly drove off the Soviet fighters and fighter-bombers.

The approach to Demyansk

The *Totenkopf* Division's advance continued, and just as the rains came, its reconnaissance battalion reached the River Pola at Vasilyevschina. Almost immediately the division's vehicles began to bog down in the mud. The *Totenkopf* Division was then hit by the Soviets before it could prepare an attack and spent two days beating off determined assaults.

A crossing of the River Pola after pressing home its advance was demanded by LVI Panzer Corps, according to orders that arrived on 30 August. SS-Brigadeführer und Generalmajor der Waffen-SS Georg Kepple, who was wounded, was only able to command the battered *Totenkopf* Division after the evacuation of Eicke temporarily. Seeing that his new command was in no fit state to attack such a well-defended line, Kepple now appealed to von Manstein, who agreed that the attack should be postponed for a few days. The Soviet attacks continued unabated so there was to be no respite for the *Totenkopf* Division.

The support of the 503rd Infantry Regiment and a brief improvement in the weather allowed the *Totenkopf* Division to throw itself over the River Pola on 5 September. However, the rains had returned again before the day was done and furious counterattacks once again were being launched by the Soviets. Two days later the weather improved, allowing the roads to begin to dry out and affording greater freedom of movement to the Germans. To slow progress again, the Soviets had planted booby traps and peppered the *Totenkopf* Division's routes with mines. By 12 September the *Totenkopf* Division was once more forced onto the defensive by the considerable stiffening of resistance and the ferocity of Soviet counterattacks.

The forests north of Demyansk had been infested by Soviet stragglers and in the middle of the month the job of clearing them fell to the *Totenkopf* Division. On 21 September command of the *Totenkopf* Division was once again in the hands of Eicke, who had returned in time to learn that intelligence was predicting a major Soviet thrust in that area and fresh enemy units were arriving to bolster Soviet strength. Probing attacks soon got underway to feel the *Totenkopf* Division's strengths and weaknesses. The offensive began at noon on 24 September, when the German lines began to be smashed by Soviet infantry, with armoured support. Firing over open sights, the *Totenkopf* Division's artillery fired round after round of high-explosive, while nine enemy tanks were knocked out courtesy of the *Totenkopf* Division's anti-tank gunners. The Soviets had been forced back out of Lushno by the close of that day by the *Totenkopf* Division's troops. However, the outlook seemed bad once more for Eicke and his men as on 26–27 September the attacks continued unabated with even greater ferocity. The *Totenkopf* Division had to weather the strength of the equivalent of three divisions, supported by 100 tanks. Such was the plight of the situation that Eicke, all his staff officers and other noncombatant personnel availed themselves of weapons and proceeded to the trenches to join their comrades. Weakened as they were, the *Totenkopf* Division's troops, demonstrating almost superhuman endeavour, threw back repeatedly an attacking force three times their own strength with the result that the Soviet attacks eventually petered out.

The exploits of Fritz Christen

The esprit de corps of the SS is demonstrated by this episode, as well as the phenomenal determination of the soldiers of the *Totenkopf* Division when faced with such overwhelming odds. SS-Unterscharführer Fritz Christen was a gunner with 2nd company SS-Antitank Detachment of the *Totenkopf* Division. His battery was located just north of Lushno, taking the full brunt of the first Soviet armoured assault on the morning of 24 September 1941. Christen was the only member of the battery to survive. He stayed at his post, firing feverishly, until he had driven off the attacking tanks, accounting for six destroyed. Christen remained alone in the emplacement for the next two days. He repeatedly repulsed Russian infantry and tank attacks with his 50mm cannon while exposed to a continual hail of

artillery, mortar and machine gun fire. Christen hung on grimly, cut off completely from the rest of his unit and the division. Refusing to abandon his post, he carried shells to his gun from the disabled batteries around him during the hours of darkness and blazed away at enemy infantry and tanks by dawn. On 27 September the Russians were finally driven out of Lushno and his astonished SS comrades found him still crouched behind his anti-tank cannon. In 72 hours he had killed nearly 100 enemy soldiers and knocked out 13 Soviet tanks. For this feat he was awarded the Knight's Cross of the Iron Cross, making him the first and also the youngest enlisted man from the ranks of the Waffen-SS to be so honoured. He was flown to the Hitler HQ at Rastenburg and received the decoration from Hitler himself.

Fighting without end

With the objective of pursuing the retreating Soviets towards the Waldai Heights, the *Totenkopf* Division resumed its march eastwards on 8 October. Samoskye had well-constructed defences 10km (6 miles) deep in places skirting it, set amid densely wooded terrain. The *Totenkopf* Division encountered these on 16 October. An offensive was launched on 17 October by the *Totenkopf* Division and 30th Infantry Division, which almost immediately foundered. In retaliation frenzied attacks were launched by the Soviets and both German divisions soon were on the defensive, fighting for their lives.

Left: Operation 'Typhoon', the codename for the attack on Moscow, began at the beginning of October 1941. But the swamp-like roads and sodden ground made progress extremely slow. The Das Reich *Division, for example, got bogged down almost straight away, and also ran into fierce resistance.*

Since the start of the campaign almost 9000 men had been lost by the *Totenkopf* Division alone, and in their weakened state it soon became clear that most other German divisions would be unable to progress any further, particularly since the weather was deteriorating with the onset of winter. The decision was therefore taken to dig in. All along this sector of the front the Germans did just that and spent the rest of that year holding off Soviet attacks and fighting partisan activity in the rear areas.

Das Reich goes into action

The 4th and 9th Armies and the 2nd and 3rd Panzer Groups were included in Army Group Centre. General Heinz Guderian's 2nd Panzer Group had the *Das Reich* Division allocated to it, serving together with the army's 10th Panzer Division the elite *Grossdeutschland* Regiment in XLVI Panzer Corps.

In the first few days of the campaign *Das Reich* was not committed to the fray. However, a river crossing between Citva and Dukova had to be forced and on 28 June *Das Reich* undertook this task. It was then to guard the northern flank of the German advance along the main road from Minsk to Smolensk. The division's engineers had constructed a temporary bridge over the River *Beresina*, which *Das Reich* reached and crossed by 4 July.

The contribution the SS-engineer units played in the early phases of the campaign in the east cannot be overstated. They enabled the Waffen-SS to accomplish the feats of

Left: By mid-November 1941, the Waffen-SS had suffered 407 officers and 7930 men killed since the start of Operation 'Barbarossa'. A further 816 officers and 26,299 of its men had been wounded – such was the price for establishing a military reputation second to none. But still the Russians were undefeated.

rapid progress it did. Without the efforts these men made, especially in constructing temporary bridges and clearing mines and other obstacles, often under heavy fire and struggling against other tortuous difficulties, it would simply not have been possible to maintain the rate of advance the SS units were able to achieve. Their comrades in the engineers were deprived of the glory that the armoured and infantry units achieved, but their missions were no less hazardous and costly in combat attrition terms. While repairing a bridge over the River Pruth, 2 Company of the engineer battalion of the *Das Reich* Division was ambushed by Soviet forces and 72 of its complement were killed, which all but wiped out the entire company– a graphic illustration of the awful situation these units endured.

An important road junction stood on the high ground east of the small town of Yelnya, situated on the River Desna. *Das Reich* set off along the main Minsk-Moscow road on 22 July to take this objective. The assault was made by the *Deutschland* and *Der Führer* Regiments, together with armour from the 10th Panzer Division. On the left wing *Deutschland*, with support of army tanks, and on the right *Der Führer*, without the benefit of artillery support, made their initial attack. The first ridge of the heights had been secured by nightfall. By the end of the day good progress had been made by *Der Führer*, which had penetrated the Soviet defensive lines.

The Soviets relinquished the high ground on the following day after the Germans continued their push. The climatic conditions had considerably weakened the Germans, as much as the losses to the enemy. A searing hot sun relentlessly beat down, baking the terrain, which, being open ground, provided little respite or welcome shade. Added to

this, supplies of water were low. The SS troops were allowed to go temporarily on the defensive by Corps Headquarters, which realised that these units could not be expected to continue the advance against a stiffening enemy resistance in the state they were now in. Vicious Soviet counterattacks soon followed, which the SS infantrymen in their state were hard pressed to repulse. Corps decision proved correct.

Fierce hand-to-hand fighting often occurred when the German positions were penetrated – usually it was the only method to drive out the Soviets. In some instances, positions changed hands two or three times before the SS troops regained complete control. The Waffen-SS gunners had received orders to fire only upon clearly defined targets, as their ammunition was beginning to run low. The attacks eventually subsided, making it possible to relieve the Waffen-SS troopers. *Das Reich* was moved south in the second week of September so it could participate in the drive to, and encirclement of, Kiev. It was still part of the 2nd Panzer Group and had been tasked with operating on the right flank of XXIV Panzer Corps.

The Pripet Marshes

In Operation 'Barbarossa's' opening phases, rapid progress during the advance through Russia had been made by German forces both to the north and south of the great Pripet Marshes. A formidable natural obstacle was formed by them, which caused a huge salient to bulge into German-held territory. At least five Soviet armies comprising around 50 divisions were concentrated within the salient. In a massive pincer movement they now had to be cut off and destroyed by the Wehrmacht. The southwest end of the salient was to be attacked by the 6th Army, which was to swing up for the purpose and draw the Soviet armies defending that area. In the north the 2nd Army with the 2nd Panzer Group formed one half of the pincer, while in the south the 17th Army with the 1st Panzer Group formed the other, trapping the Soviet armies when they linked up to the east of Kiev.

During the rapid drive south the *Das Reich* Division was ordered to take the vital bridge at Makoshim over the River Desna, with the Luftwaffe's Stukas giving air support. On reaching the approaches to the river, *Das Reich* could see the opposite bank was well defended. The Waffen-SS commanders waited in vain for their air support and then decided to attack without it. A high-speed dash over the bridge was made by motorcycle troops from the

reconnaissance battalion and the defenders, taken by surprise, were engaged in close combat. Meanwhile, the wires to the demolition charges were frantically being cut by other units on the bridge and it was captured completely intact. Belatedly, the Luftwaffe's Stukas arrived and began to dive-bomb the SS troops who were securing their bridgehead against potential counterattacks, killing 40 Waffen-SS soldiers into the bargain.

Das Reich now began driving south in the direction of Priluki, Borsna and the crossings at the River Uday. On 15 September Kiev was completely encircled, the SS infantry having successfully seized their previous objectives. The Soviet Red Army units made frantic

attempts to break out of the encirclement, but the Germans beat back all of their entrapped victims' efforts. Losses in the Kiev pocket amounted to a staggering tally of over one million Soviet troops either killed or captured.

On 4 October Operation 'Typhoon', the attack on Moscow, began, with progress initially being excellent. *Das Reich*, accompanied by the 10th Panzer Division, advanced but with

Below: As 1941 came to an end, the Waffen-SS continued to battle through the winter snows to reach their objectives. By this stage of the campaign, many generals were glad to have Waffen-SS units under their command, especially as Russian resistance was hardening and the Red Army was launching counterattacks.

Above: Das Reich *personnel on the march during Operation 'Typhoon', the attack on Moscow. On 4 December, soldiers of the division's Reconnaissance Battalion actually reached the outer fringes of the city. But two days later Zhukov's massive counterattack began. Moscow was saved and the Waffen-SS faced a long, hard winter.*

the advent of the autumn rains the division was rapidly bogged down, the roads being quickly transformed into swamps, and it only reached Gzhatsk on 9 October. Temperatures plummeted dramatically, bringing the first of countless numbers of frostbite cases that were to afflict the troops. The Russian winter climate was now a major factor as the troops were inadequately protected against it. By mid-October, meeting fierce resistance, *Das Reich* was on the move again, pushing along the main road to Moscow. On 18 October it crossed the River Moskva, and the town of Mozhaisk fell to the division.

From late October until mid-November the Germans concentrated on consolidating their gains. Supplies of ammunition were running low, impeding offensive opera-

tions, and another major factor was that the weather conditions had worsened. On 18 November XLVI Panzer Corps was ordered to continue its advance, making a thrust towards Istra. After fierce fighting, the town was finally penetrated on 26 November by the remaining tanks of 10th Panzer Division and *Das Reich.*

The division still held the hope of pushing on towards Moscow itself, but with every day that passed the weather conditions were becoming more severe. Both the *Deutschland* and *Der Führer* regiments had to be regrouped as the loss in manpower had been so great, one battalion from each being disbanded and the men redistributed. The freezing temperatures were not just taking a toll on men – vehicles suffered too. All but seven of the tanks of the 10th Panzer Division had been rendered inoperable due to arctic conditions and the enhanced mechanical wear and tear they caused.

The Moscow city tramcar system terminus was reached on 4 December 1941. This was achieved by troops of *Das Reich*'s reconnaissance battalion before the weather

closed in and forced a pause in the attack. In the assault on Moscow this was to be the furthest point reached. On 6 December 1941, in the region of one and a half million Soviet troops, numbering 17 whole armies, hurled themselves against an exhausted German force. The Soviet winter offensive began. The order to retreat was given on 9 December, and as the long weary trek westwards started, *Das Reich* began to retire.

The Waffen-SS had shown it could match anything the German army could field during the Eastern Front's first campaign. Few in the military hierarchy would now question the value of a combat soldier of the Waffen-SS. However, resentment and grave suspicions concerning the 'political' nature of Himmler's troops were still harboured by many. The Waffen-SS had speedily acquired a reputation for fanatical endeavour and heroism that few other units could equal and this fact was beyond all doubt. Yet the incautious attitudes of many Waffen-SS officers were still a cause for concern, for it was felt that this led to excessive casualties in their units.

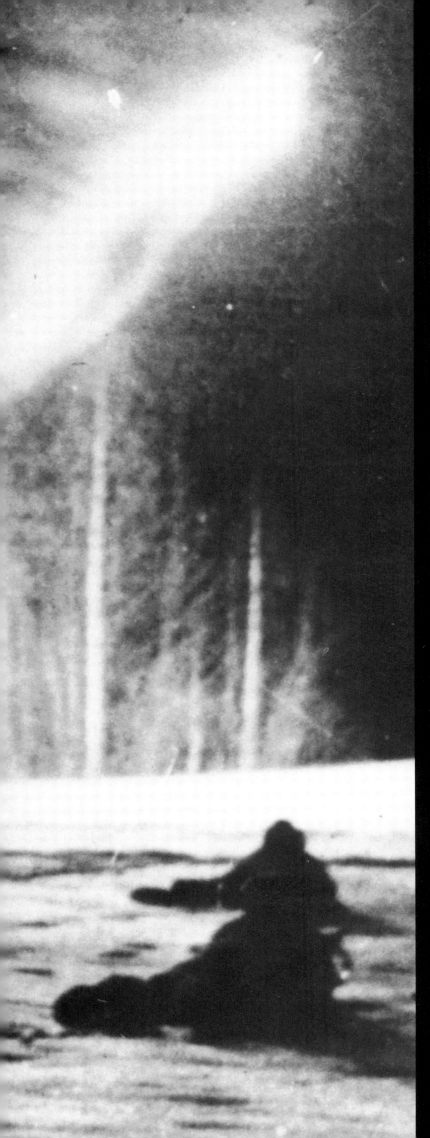

CHAPTER 6

DEATH
AT DEMYANSK

By Hitler's own reckoning, the bravery of the *Totenkopf* Division in the Demyansk Pocket in 1942 was the driving element among the German formations that held on in northern Russia and which saved the whole front from collapse. As usual the Waffen-SS fought fanatically, but Eicke's division emerged from the battles as mere shadows of their former selves, and many thousands gave their lives in suicidal attempts to halt the Russian advance.

Left: Totenkopf *soldiers in the Demyansk Pocket in January 1942. Contrary to popular opinion, Waffen-SS troops were supplied with adequate winter clothing in 1941-42.*

Left: On the lookout for the next Russian attack on the edge of the pocket. By the beginning of February 1942, the Totenkopf *Division had been divided into two battle groups, which were deployed in the two most hard-pressed areas inside the pocket. For Eicke's men it was a new kind of war: one of primitive survival.*

what was soon to be called the Demyansk Pocket.

The Soviet Red Army's fresh, well-equipped divisions were poised on the 5 December to be unleashed by Marshal Zhukov against Army Group Centre. The exhausted German soldiers began to crack almost immediately and the lines buckled. Hitler was adamant that every German soldier was to stand firm. Ironically, Hitler's inflexibility helped to avert a total rout of the German armies before Moscow, as the German defences firmed up gradually. The end of January 1942 saw the front stabilised, and in the central sector the Soviet offensive exhausted itself.

The 16th Army in danger

Soviet forces were massing to the north, the objective of Soviet strategy being to encircle and annihilate the German 16th Army. Army Group North and Army Group Centre would then have a vast space between them, which would permit the Red Army to flow through. The southern shore of Lake Ilmen was the intended advance route for the Soviet 11th and 34th Armies, and the 1st Shock Army. Aiming to sweep around the lower edge of Lake Seliger, the 16th Shock Army also advanced to join the other thrust.

German intelligence had been alerted by reports from reconnaissance flights of large-scale Soviet troop movements, and Soviet forces building up in the north had also been detected. In the north, German forces were accordingly permitted the advantage of arranging their

By early December 1941, having endured six months of continuous fighting, mounting casualties, horrendous weather and supply lines which were over-stretched, the Germans were close to the brink of collapse in Russia. On the whole the troops were still equipped with little more than summer uniforms, and now the full horrors of the Russian winter were being visited upon them. Although the very gates of Moscow itself had been rattled by

the Germans, the Red Army, albeit having been pushed far back, was able to establish a reserve to the east of the Soviet capital. As the winter's first blizzard blew its icy breath, the Germans found themselves locked in the deadly embrace of the first major Soviet counteroffensive, which smashed into the German lines and tore huge gaps in the front. The *Totenkopf* Division, with five other German divisions, was destined to find itself cut off in

defence strategies. During December, the Germans concentrated their efforts on the defence lines, strengthening and firming them up. Two German corps – II Corps and X Corps – were positioned in the area between Lake Ilmen and Lake Seliger, and along the Lovat river to the west. Under the command of SS-Obergruppenführer Theodor Eicke, the *Totenkopf* Division was part of this force, and during December had dug itself in around the Valdai Hills.

During the night of the 7/8 January 1942, Zhukov launched the second phase of his winter counter-offensive under cover of a fierce blizzard. The Red Army's attack was along the whole of Army Group North's southern flank. The 30th and 290th Infantry Divisions, the *Totenkopf*'s neighbours, received the full brunt of the 11th Army, 34th Army and 1st Shock Army. The Soviet forces pierced the German lines in places by up to 32km (20 miles) and all but annihilated the two divisions.

The Soviets put into action a plan to trap the 16th Army. Staraya Russa was chosen by the 11th Army as the point at which to turned south into the rear of II Corps, and it had advanced that far by 9 January. From the shores of Lake Seliger, driving west with the intention of linking up with the 11th Army and 1st Shock Army, the 16th Shock Army then turned north along the line of the River Lovat.

The *Totenkopf* is deployed

On the orders of the 16th Army, the *Totenkopf* Division was divided and deployed to various crisis points. This resulted in two infantry battalions being sent to Demyansk with the objective of strengthening the 16th Army's flanks. Staraya Russa was chosen for the *Totenkopf* Division's reconnaissance battalions of infantry, which they were ordered to hold at all costs. These segregated deployments of the division were much to Eicke's displeasure.

Field Marshal Leeb perceived that the situation had become so critical by 12 January 1942 that the best course of action was to form a new defensive line and withdraw both his corps over the River Lovat. He was certain that if the 16th Army stood firm it would be totally destroyed. Leeb asked Hitler's permission to withdraw, but he refused, ordering his troops to hold fast. An outraged Leeb asked to be relieved of his command; Hitler agreed and replaced him with Colonel-General Küchler, the former commander of the 18th Army, who replaced Leeb on 17 January.

Meanwhile, the two German corps' situation had continued to

Til vakt ved Nordens grense mot øst!

⚡⚡-SKIJEGERBATALJON NORGE

Left: A recruiting poster for Norwegian Waffen-SS recruits, a somewhat romanticised image of fighting on the Eastern Front. During the first winter on the front, for example, there were many cases of frostbite among German units, with many losing fingers to what the Russians called 'General Winter'.

deteriorate, resulting in them slowly being constricted into a pocket centred around Demyansk On 20 January, the Soviet armies had broken through along the River Lovat, which was a setback for Colonel-General Küchler's command, by now only three days old. The German units were now separated on the west and east banks of the river. The Soviets took heavy losses at Staraya Russa at the hands of the *Totenkopf* elements and the army's 18th Motorised Division, who held the position.

Despite the German divisions' determined resistance in the Valdai region, given Hitler's orders and Soviet strength, it was only a matter of time before the encirclement of a major portion of the 16th Army became inevitable. For another three weeks heavy fighting continued as the Soviets gradually closed the ring. About 40km (25 miles) west of Demyansk, units of the

Soviet 11th and 1st Shock armies linked up on the River Lovat on 8 February. The Soviet ring had closed firmly around II and X Corps, trapping the 12th, 30th, 32nd, 123rd and 290th Infantry Divisions, plus the remainder of the *Totenkopf* Division. The Soviets had to hand the equivalent of 15 fresh infantry divisions, well equipped, supported by an assortment of armoured units and independent ski battalions, pressing in on the exhausted and badly battered Germans. Inside the pocket there were 95,000 men and 20,000 horses. Göring, commander of the Luftwaffe, assured Hitler that with the total collapse of the supply lines it could be supplied by air, the responsibility for which the Luftwaffe would undertake. Hitler once again reiterated his orders forbidding any attempt to break out to the west. The trapped German divisions were instructed to stand firm and hold their positions until a new

front was built west of the River Lovat and a relief attack launched to rescue them.

An estimated supply of nearly 200 tonnes (197 tons) would be required to supply the pocket. Weapons, ammunition, food and medicines had to be brought in by air, and Göring's supply operations at its peak actually reached a total of just under 300 tonnes (295 tons) daily. Initially at least, the Luftwaffe's transport squadrons were able to more than match the daily requirements of the pocket's defenders. These drop achievements were not sustainable, though, and they gradu-

Below: A Panzer III in northern Russia in 1942. Unlike in the Blitzkrieg, the Germans in the Demyansk Pocket had to fight a new kind of war: a defensive campaign. The odds were formidable: two trapped German Army Corps – 95,000 men – were surrounded by 15 Red Army divisions at full strength.

Left: Totenkopf *soldiers enjoy the luxury of a brief pause between Red Army assaults. At one point in February and early March Eicke's battle group held out for a month in chest-high snow and sub-zero temperatures. Such was the calibre of the Waffen-SS soldiers that they were able to repulse the enemy attacks.*

of the Red Army. These penetrations had produced their own little pockets as individual villages were cut off and surrounded. Losses were mounting dramatically for the *Totenkopf* Division, but it still held doggedly to its objective. The situation on the ground had become so confused that the Waffen-SS troops were strafed by their own side as other Luftwaffe aircraft dropped supplies right into the laps of the Soviet attackers.

The frenzied assault on the German positions was undertaken by even more fresh Soviet divisions. This involved prolonged and bitter fighting, with both sides giving no quarter. Eicke appealed directly to Himmler for replacements, now fearing for the very survival of his fragmented and mauled division. When Himmler was eventually able to muster several hundred replacements that could be flown into the pocket, the Luftwaffe insisted that its supply flights had not the capacity to carry them.

Crisis point

Soviet troops had so widely infiltrated Eicke's sector that all contact with neighbouring German units had been lost by the end of February. Feeling that everything was hopeless and the annihilation of his battle group imminent, as it now only numbered some 1460 officers and men, Eicke signalled his desperate situation to II Corps.

In this period the Soviet attacks became even more desperate because the coming spring thaw would turn the frozen battleground

ally dropped off, with the Luftwaffe struggling to meet even half the estimated requirements. Before the supply lines were cut, the *Totenkopf* Division's supply officers had procured for their troops an ample supply of warm winter clothing though SS channels. This was one thing that helped the division's soldiers.

General Brockdorff-Ahlefeldt took command of the troops within the pocket once the Soviet ring around Demyansk finally closed. Eicke was further infuriated when the remaining *Totenkopf* units within the pocket were split into two battle groups, which were constructed from *Totenkopf* and army personnel. Eicke commanded the larger group, and was ordered to defend the southwest sector of the pocket. This involved the protection of a large network of villages and their interlinking roads. The principal task entrusted to Eicke and his command was to hold firm in their

sector. The German units on the eastern and western banks of the River Lovat had had a corridor driven between them, which had to be prevented from being widened by the Soviets at all costs. SS-Oberführer Max Simon commanded the second battle group, which was positioned in the northeastern edge of the pocket, facing the Soviet 34th Army.

To deny any form of shelter to the *Totenkopf* troops, incendiary bombs were dropped by the Red Army Air Force wherever a building stood. They were fighting in sub-zero temperatures and in snow well over one metre (3.28ft) deep. The pressure from all areas that Eicke's battle group was subjected to was intense as it tried to hold its line of scattered villages. By late February, the German lines had been penetrated in a number of places by Russian forces. Eicke's men had also been incessantly pounded by the artillery

Below: A Panzer IV equipped with side skirts and a long-barrelled 75mm gun. The Panzer IV performed well in both army and Waffen-SS service on all fronts throughout the war. It was continually updated, modifications including more armour to defeat anti-tank weapons.

into a muddy quagmire which would bog down their operations, disadvantaging the attackers far more than the defenders. Every effort therefore had to be made to crush the Demyansk Pocket before this happened.

The dire situation the *Totenkopf* Division now found itself in was brought to Hitler's notice by Himmler. Hitler gave the orders to have the replacements flown into the pocket as soon as possible. The Luftwaffe, due to an improvement in weather conditions, was permitted to make a substantial drop to the beleaguered defenders of essential ammunition, food and medicines, and on 7 March the fresh *Totenkopf* Division troops finally arrived at Demyansk.

In mid-March, as the spring thaws set in, the Soviet attacks began to tail off. In their attempt to annihilate the Demyansk Pocket, the Soviets had suffered well over 20,000 casualties, while during the same period the *Totenkopf* Division had lost around 7000 men. The Soviets never had a problem with regards to short-

ages of manpower, as their losses could quickly be made good. For the Germans it was different: in the case of the *Totenkopf* Division losses of 7000 were replaced by only 5000 men.

The relief force

Meanwhile, Lieutenant-General Walter von Seydlitz-Kurzbach assembled under his command a relief force. On the west bank of the River Lovat from the beginning of March 1942 there had been a build-up of German forces which he was now to employ: the 5th and 8th Light Divisions, and 122nd, 127th and 329th Infantry Divisions. Their objective was to drive eastwards over the River Lovat towards the pocket, while Eicke's battle group would wait to be given a signal to make a corresponding push to the west when the time was ripe. The codenamed Operation 'Fallreep' was employed for the relief of the Demyansk Pocket.

Supported by massive air power, the offensive began on 21 March and good progress was made for the first

two days. Progress slowed as the Soviet resistance began to stiffen, with the Russians frantically battling to prevent a link-up between the German forces. It was not until two weeks after the push eastwards had begun that Seydlitz-Kurzbach felt confident enough to give Eicke his orders to begin his attack westwards. The delay meant the spring thaw would once more turn the ground into boggy marshland, through which Eicke's troops would have to trudge yet again. The Soviets were attacked with a frenzied determination by the Waffen-SS infantry, with vicious hand-to-hand combat often resulting. Due to stiff Soviet resistance and the horrendous conditions, a rate of advance of only around 1.6km (one mile) per day was managed by the men of the *Totenkopf* Division.

The east bank of the River Lovat was reached by a company from the *Totenkopf* Division's tank-destroyer battalion on 20 April, and on the following day it was joined by the remainder of the battle group. The bridgehead over the River Lovat was sufficiently secured after 73 days to start moving into what had now become the Demyansk salient, and Seydlitz-Kurzbach dispatched the first troops and supplies into it on 22 April 1943.

However, the *Totenkopf* Division's ordeal was far from being over. The remnants of Eicke's once mighty division, it was hoped, would be pulled out of the front, to be given the chance to recover, as they were now in a dreadful physical state, also that the division might undergo extensive rebuilding and refitting. Hitler, with scant regard for their condition, ordered that they remain in the salient. Their task was to see that the German corridor was held open, for it was thought it would soon come under renewed attack.

Within the western part of the salient, all SS and army troops came under Eicke's command and were to be combined into a new 'corps'. This formation in reality had the total strength of around only half that of a single fully manned division. Colonel-General Busch was consulted by Eicke, who made his pessimism concerning the *Totenkopf*'s situation known. Having first-hand knowledge of the appalling condition of countless numbers of the members of the *Totenkopf* Division, Busch was very sympathetic. Personally interceding, he stated that Eicke's exhausted corps must have an immediate intake of at least 5000 fresh troops if it was to continue with its allotted tasks. But a further 3000 replacements was all that was to be sent in the end by Himmler.

Renewed Red Army attacks

The new corridor came under attack and was only held open with great difficulty when the Red Army once again went over to the offensive in May 1942. Through the month and into early summer the Soviet actions grew in determination and strength as their build-up continued. The SS troops, now totally exhausted, had no chance for any form of rest. The frequency of Soviet attacks and constant attrition through these defensive actions significantly weakened Eicke's corps. The commander himself was also now exhausted.

SS-Oberführer Max Simon was given temporary command of the *Totenkopf* Division in mid-June, when Eicke was ordered to take a spell of leave. Eicke was ordered to report to the Führer Headquarters at Rastenburg at the end of his spell of leave, where Hitler personally decorated him with the Oakleaves to his Knight's Cross, becoming the eighty-eighth recipient. Eicke, in private conversation with Hitler, plainly described the appaling state of his remaining troops.

Expressing his sympathy, Hitler refused just yet to allow the *Totenkopf* Division to be withdrawn from Demyansk However, he did promise that when the division eventually was withdrawn, Eicke would see it become a fully rebuilt

Below: A section of Totenkopf *Division soldiers gather supplies dropped by the Luftwaffe into the Demyansk Pocket. Göring's transport aircraft failed to get more than half the minimum requirements to the trapped German forces inside the pocket, the result of poor weather and the activity of Russian aircraft.*

Left: In a formal award ceremony held at Rastenburg on 26 June 1942, in which Theodor Eicke was awarded the Oak Leaves to his Knight's Cross, Hitler praised him and the men of the Totenkopf *Division, stating that it was they who had maintained the pocket throughout the winter and had thus saved the front.*

The exhausted *Totenkopf* troops were once more subjected to massive Soviet assaults, which smashed into the Waffen-SS units on 17 July. Sustaining considerable losses, these attacks were only held back by fanatical Waffen-SS determination. Vasilyevschina was captured by the Red Army on 18 July, with its *Totenkopf* Division defenders wiped out to a man. In a mind-boggling act of insubordination, Simon flatly refused to launch an immediate counterattack, in contradiction of orders from his army superiors. Instead, he suggested that they should do it themselves if the army required the task to be done. The corps command presumably must have appreciated the poor condition of the Waffen-SS troops, for the refusal to obey the order to assault brought no repercussions for Simon. The attack was indeed carried out, with the army sending in its own troops. The *Totenkopf* Division was replaced for the mission by the 8th Light Division, which suffered heavy losses and still failed to oust the Soviets in the process.

The exhausted Waffen-SS

Attempts by the Soviets to crush the salient continued in weather conditions that can only be described as atrocious. Men of both sides, thigh-deep in glutinous mud, fought for several days until eventually the Soviet attacks eased off, on 30 July. Both sides had fought themselves to an exhausted standstill. Literally on their last legs, Simon's exhausted troops were suffering the results of long periods of fighting in what can

and reformed panzergrenadier (armoured infantry division), complete with its own tank battalion. A further order was given that until the division was withdrawn from the front, Eicke was to remain on leave in Germany.

By early July the *Totenkopf* Division was under severe Soviet pressure, which was building up once again in the areas it defended. The removal of the division was desperately pleaded for by Simon before it was destroyed, as the anni-

hilation of the division was only a matter of time in his opinion. But his pleadings were to no avail. After having read Simon's reports, Eicke begged once more for the withdrawal of his division. Until the salient had been sufficiently strengthened, though, by the German X Corps, which was estimated would take at least a further six to eight weeks, Hitler insisted that the remnants of the *Totenkopf* Division would not be released and must stand firm no matter what its condition.

only be described as swamp conditions. Diseases spread among the shattered remnants of the *Totenkopf* Division like wildfire, the soldiers succumbing easily to dysentery, pneumonia and many other racking complaints.

Eicke once again presented himself to Hitler in an attempt to register his anger that his division had been left to wallow in these conditions. He demanded that the division be withdrawn from the Demyansk salient so that it could rest and undergo a complete refit, or else he should be allowed to return to the front, where if necessary he might die with his men. Hitler, not surprisingly, refused. Eicke was ordered instead to take long-term convalescent leave.

Debilitating casualties were once again suffered by the *Totenkopf*

Division, when both the northern and southern edges of the corridor came under heavy attacks launched on 6 August by the Soviet 11th Army and I Guards Corps. Conspicuously absent, the Luftwaffe gave the freedom of the skies to the Soviet Red Army Air Force, which could strafe and bomb at will while massed artillery barrages were poured on the SS troops. By 12 August, there were no reserves left whatsoever. The trenches had been filled with all the *Totenkopf* non-combatant personnel who had been armed. Clerks, medics, police and cooks joined their comrades in the trenches.

The heavens opened, delivering torrential rains, and for two days the weather was so atrocious that all military operations ceased. This saved the *Totenkopf* Division from the very real likelihood of being

overrun by the Red Army and also afforded a brief time to regroup.

On 25 August, the 7th guards division, 129th, 130th, 364th and 391st infantry divisions and the 30th rifle brigade mounted massive attacks. Simon's command determinedly held its positions, but lost over 1000 men in just a few hours. At last, in October 1942, the *Totenkopf* was finally withdrawn, with only 6400 soldiers still remaining alive. Thus came to an end one of the most epic actions of World War II.

Below: Totenkopf *soldiers on the attack in mid-1942. By this time around one-third of the division's troops were underweight, weak and listless, due to lack of food, intense cold and inadequate winter shelter. The division was finally withdrawn from the front for rest and refitting – but it would soon be back.*

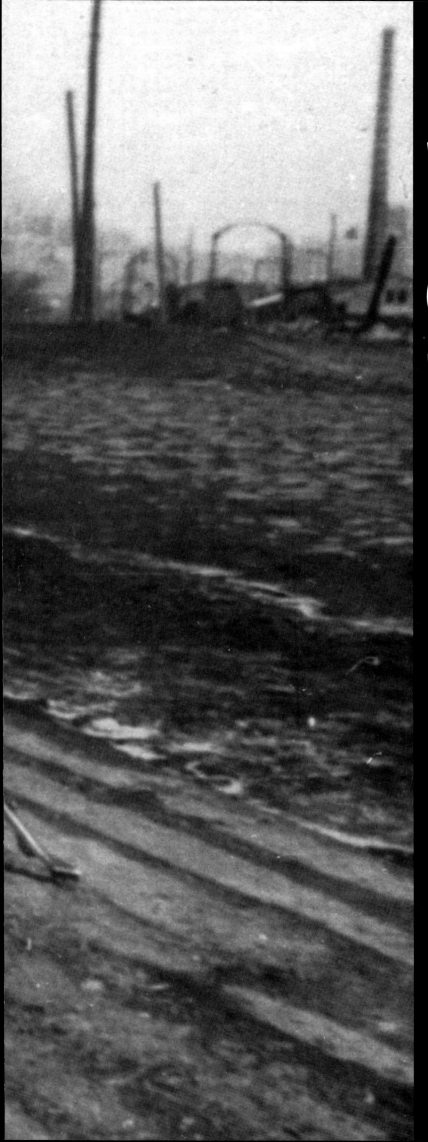

CHAPTER 7

WINTER STORM

In January 1943 the Red Army
launched a winter offensive that
smashed the German front in
southern Russia. All seemed lost,
but in a dazzling counterattack the
newly formed I SS Panzer Corps
retook Kharkov and inflicted a
heavy defeat upon the Red Army.
The Russian onslaught was
stopped in its tracks, and a jubilant
Hitler looked to his elite Waffen-SS
divisions to win the war in Russia.

*Left: Waffen-SS soldiers fighting in the suburbs of Kharkov in
March 1943. Well equipped and clothed, the men of I SS Panzer
Corps were more than a match for the Russian defenders.*

Left: A knocked-out Russian T-34 lies abandoned near Kharkov. By the middle of February 1943, the momentum that had carried the Red Army to the city was spent. Its supply lines were over-extended, its units weakened and its soldiers exhausted. It was the perfect time for Manstein to launch his counterattack.

hours. Hausser was adamant that he would not consider the annihilation of his corps in the hopeless endeavour to save Kharkov, stating: 'It is already settled, Kharkov is being evacuated.'

The Red Army stalls

When Hitler learned that his personal order had been disregarded he flew into one of his uncontrollable rages and demanded to be flown to Field Marshal von Manstein's Army Group South headquarters at Zaporozhye for an explanation. Meanwhile, the corridor out of Kharkov had contracted to a mere 1.6km (one mile) wide at the most, and it was along this that Hausser's troops had to go in order to escape to German-held ground farther west. The action was carried out in the nick of time. The taking of this strategic city gave the Soviets a sense of achievement, but this was soon tempered as the momentum of their offensive faltered. Their forces were exhausted: the German defence had been so tenacious that it had brought about a large loss of life, which had to be replaced.

Kharkov, Hitler ordered, must be retaken. He stated that the Soviets could easily be ejected. The arrival of the *Totenkopf* Division was imminent, and thus reinforced I SS Panzer Corps could launch an immediate counterattack. Field Marshal von Manstein had other plans for I SS Panzer Corps, which he wished to employ as the upper claw in a large pincer movement which had as its objective the encirclement and destruction of the

In January 1943, the elite divisions of the Waffen-SS, the *Leibstandarte, Das Reich* and *Totenkopf*, were grouped together in I SS Panzer Corps. These divisions were refitting in the West, but were rushed to the southern sector of the Eastern Front in an attempt to stem the Red tide. Under the command of SS-Obergruppenführer 'Papa' Hausser, the *Leibstandarte* and *Das Reich* were grouped around Kharkov. Hitler, in his inimitable manner, gave the order that it was to be held at all costs. In the city, Hausser received the order and took defensive actions. To be effective, the defence lines had to be shortened, but in his heart he knew Kharkov was doomed. He therefore ordered the destruction of all military installations so they did not fall into Russian hands when the city eventually fell. Enemy attacks on the eastern and southern defences of the city were putting escalating pressure on the defenders and their col-

lapse was imminent. A pointless defence of an undefendable city to Hausser, a realist, and the destruction of his command in the execution of his orders was unthinkable.

Kharkov's suburbs were probed and penetrated on the evening of 14 February by the Russians, I SS Panzer Corps' rear area being infiltrated during the next 24 hours.

The Soviet drive was temporarily stemmed when, to the northwest of Kharkov, a counterattack was launched by elements of *Das Reich*, which inflicted heavy casualties on the Russians.

Permission was once more requested to withdraw from the city so that Hausser could regroup his corps. This was placed around midday on the 15 February. With no reply being forthcoming by 1250 hours, Hausser ordered a breakout and informed army group headquarters at 1300 hours of his decision. The expected order to hold Kharkov at all costs was received at 1630

Soviet armies that were moving towards the River Dnieper.

From its position east of Dnepropetrovsk, XLVIII Panzer Corps pushed towards the River Samara with the task of securing bridgeheads across it. German morale soared when the Soviet troops retreated northwards in near panic, the unexpected German push having taken them by surprise. On the move once more were the *Totenkopf* and *Das Reich* Divisions, vacating their positions around Poltava and pushing towards the southeast. The rear of the Soviet 6th Army received a hammer blow from them, which was executed in appalling conditions: deep snow and dense fog. General Hermann Hoth, commanding the 4th Panzer Army,

would form the lower claw of the pincer. The first objective, Hitler commanded, was the retaking of Kharkov. Hitler's plan was to be thwarted, though, as an unexpected thaw had completely bogged down the *Totenkopf* Division (for the plan to work the division would have had to move off the roads and travel across country).

Field Marshal von Manstein's alternative plan was now begrudgingly approved by Hitler, and almost immediately the German counterattack got under way. The area around Krasnograd was the objective of *Das Reich*, which fell to the Waffen-SS. Peretschepino was the next target, which was quickly taken. Luftwaffe Stuka ground-attack aircraft supported *Das Reich* on 22

February as it moved towards Pavlograd. The division, fully motorised, confronted Soviet cavalry units wielding sabres. The result was slaughter as the German thrust rolled inexorably onwards. On 24 February, Pavlograd succumbed to the might of the Waffen-SS. German territorial gains were so fast that numerous 'friendly fire' actions resulted in German troops attacking their own men.

Below: SS-Obergruppenführer 'Sepp' Dietrich (left), commander of the Leibstandarte *Division. Dietrich's men held the line around Chegavayev in late January and early February 1943. While shattered Italian, German and Hungarian units streamed past it, Hitler's bodyguard stood like a rock against the Red Army.*

Swinging to the northeast after the two divisions had joined forces, *Totenkopf* and *Das Reich* drove parallel to the retreating line of Soviets and raked it with fire, causing immense casualties. The Waffen-SS troops found that where Soviet units became short on fuel they simply left their vehicles, causing long immobile columns of tanks, trucks and other transport all in full working order.

What happened in the ensuing days to the demoralised Soviet forces was little more than slaughter. Two Soviet armies were destroyed, and 600 enemy tanks were either captured or destroyed. In fact, the haul was so great that a full tank detachment of recovered T-34s was able to be utilised by *Das Reich*. To this catalogue of success was added 600 anti-tank guns and in excess of 400 artillery pieces. Not so impressive, however, was the quantity of Soviet personnel eradicated: 9000 were captured and 23,000 killed. The reason for this was that the Soviet troops abandoned their heavy equipment and made good

their escape on foot, finding gaps in the German line, which they were able to filter through in small groups. The Germans also suffered casualties that were not inconsiderable. Possibly the most notable was the loss of the former concentration camp inspector, SS-Obergruppen-führer Theodor Eicke, killed on 26 February 1943.

Above: The Totenkopf *Division rumbles into Kharkov. The division had enveloped the area to the north of the city between 11 and 15 March and had captured the vital bridge over the Donetz at Chuguyev. As it did so it ran into the elite Soviet 25th Guards Rifle Division and annihilated it in savage fighting.*

The Soviet High Command, STAVKA, in order to block any pushes towards Kharkov by the Germans, deployed more troops into the sector, with the area south of the city receiving an armoured corps. However, the Germans had set a trap that these fresh Soviet troops fell straight into. Under orders from Hausser, the *Leibstandarte* had quickly established defensive positions in the Soviets' rear, and it was towards these the *Totenkopf* and *Das Reich* levered the Soviets. The enemy was totally crushed by the *Leibstandarte*'s guns and armour, which included Tiger tanks. Kharkov now lay open to the Germans.

The assault on the city came with I SS Panzer Corps and the 4th Panzer Army joining forces on 4 March. The *Leibstandarte* drove to Valki on the River Mscha, with the objective of forcing a bridgehead

Left: Cheerful panzer crews of the Das Reich *Division take the opportunity to get a bite to eat during their attack on Kharkov in March 1943. Field Marshal von Manstein had timed his counterattack to perfection, and in just one week of fighting alone the Soviet 6th Army lost over 23,000 men killed.*

across it. On the *Leibstandarte*'s left flank stood the *Totenkopf* Division, which had taken Stary Mertschyk and then driven on, taking Olshany on 9 March. On the *Leibstandarte*'s right flank stood *Das Reich*, which found that it had to battle against atrocious terrain, though its advance units still reached the outskirts of Kharkov on 9 March. The *Leibstandarte* took Peretdinaga and Polevaya on the eve of 9 March.

An attack on Kharkov from the west was now the objective the *Das Reich* Division was ordered to undertake. The defence encountered was light when *Das Reich* penetrated the outskirts of the city first, but then stiffened.

To the north, pushing down the main Belgorod-Kharkov road, SS-Panzergrenadier Regiment 1, under the command of SS-Standarten-führer Fritz Witt, smashed its way into Kharkov. SS-Panzergrenadier

Left: Street fighting in Kharkov. On 11 March Paul Hausser sent the Das Reich *and* Leibstandarte *Divisions into the city to take it by direct assault. The result was three days of vicious street fighting in which the SS suffered 11,500 casualties.*

Below: Leibstandarte *vehicles in Kharkov in mid-March 1943. The retaking of the city had convinced Hitler that his Waffen-SS divisions were invincible. He boasted that the 'SS Panzer Corps is worth 20 Italian divisions.'*

Regiment 2 was on Witt's right, commanded by SS-Standartenführer Theodor 'Teddi' Wisch. SS-Obersturmbannführer Kurt Meyer took up the left flank. 'Panzermeyer' was tasked with cutting the road from

Kharkov to Liptsy, north of the city. He decided that it would be better to travel through the woods. However, his armoured vehicles began to make heavy weather of the new terrain, and Meyer was beginning to have second thoughts when he discovered sled tracks and decided to follow them. The tracks soon narrowed, and on many occasions the column was forced to halt to enable the vehicles, which were in danger of becoming stuck, to be manhandled through the obstacles. Meyer decided that he must catch up with SS-Obersturmführer Gerd Bremer, who commanded the forward element of his command. He found him

in a clearing, at the foot of which stood a main road on which Red Army soldiers were massed in their thousands, complete with tanks and artillery. Meyer had only a handful of light vehicles and a command of just over 20 men.

The Germans then heard the engines of Stuka dive-bombers. The planes bombed and strafed the Soviet column, which was thrown into disarray. Meyer ordered his minuscule force immediately into the attack at the same time as his lead tanks came into view. The Russians panicked. Some tried unsuccessfully to flee, while many others decided to put up their hands to surrender. Hundreds of prisoners fell into the Germans' hands, and Meyer's column, hoping to maximise the element of surprise, drove to Kharkov with all the speed they could muster.

The Waffen-SS enters Kharkov

Without encountering further incident, the SS soldiers reached the city's northern outskirts. They maintained their rapid progress until they came to the edge of the city, where Meyer called a halt. Meyer and his command retraced their steps to the earlier battleground where the countless Soviet prisoners, who seemed relieved to be out of the conflict, were being supervised by a handful of grenadiers. The other members of Meyer's battalion arrived during the next few hours. The force was regrouped by dawn the following day and the advance resumed. Meyer gave the order to dig in on 11 March, as further progress was impossible due to the major problem of a shortage of fuel. A graveyard was Meyer's unusual choice, but unknown to him the main Russian escape route out of the city was situated alongside his force. During the next few hours the Waffen-SS troops repulsed numerous attempt by the Soviets to over-

run their positions. The road to the north of the city had been cut by the Soviets, news of which was brought to him when a fuel tanker was able to get through to his group. His escape route was now gone, but he learnt that the centre of the city had been penetrated by Fritz Witt's regiment, which had seized the psychologically important Red Square. No other course of action presented itself to Meyer other than to drive onwards into the city itself.

The Soviet units in the city, now caught by the impending German

Above: Waffen-SS troops in Kharkov. The victory had led to a renewed spirit of optimism in Hitler, as he realised that the SS's efforts had allowed him to plan for a new summer offensive in the East, which would be aimed at eradicating the huge Russian salient around Kursk. For the Waffen-SS, it meant much more fighting.

advance, put up a fanatical opposition in their attempts to battle their way out to the north. On the other hand, Meyer was stridently trying to hold the Soviet units who were frantically trying to evade capture. The

city's western side was being penetrated by the *Das Reich* Division, and on 12 March the main railway station had been reached in the very heart of Kharkov. SS-Sturmbannführer Peiper and his panzergrenadier battalion gave welcome relief to Meyer and his reconnaissance group situated to Kharkov's north. Together with the objective of flushing out what remained of the Soviet defenders they smashed their path to the east and southeastern sectors. Kharkov was now in the Germans' hands, and Peiper and his men raced towards Belgorod, which fell to him on 18 March 1943. This also enabled the Waffen-SS to link up with army's elite *Grossdeutschland* Division.

Above: SS-Reichsführer Heinrich Himmler (right) with the commander of I SS Panzer Corps, Paul Hausser, following the retaking of Kharkov. In a typical display of pettiness, Hitler delayed including Hausser in the list of medal winners as a punishment for his originally disobeying the Führer, when he abandoned the city in February to avoid being encircled and wiped out.

The Soviet units which had cut the Kharkov-Belgorod road were confronted by the *Totenkopf* Panzers, which destroyed them. The Germans' swing around the north of the city was continued southeast to Tshuguyev, where they captured the Donetz crossing. The *Totenkopf* Division had to repulse Soviet units fleeing from Kharkov during the next few days, as well as having to cope with fresh Soviet formations to the east launching counterattacks against them. All this effort brought little comfort to the Soviet High Command, for during these battles they saw the annihilation of their 25th Guards Rifle Division.

Black Knight victory

The Waffen-SS had won a great victory with the retaking of Kharkov but at a great price: over 11,500 of its members having been killed. After the three days of fanatical close-quarter fighting in the city, which gave the prize to the Waffen-SS, Hitler now perceived his political warriors in an even more invincible light.

The Kharkov victory forged the reputation of fearless Waffen-SS heroism in attack and steadfastness in defence. Adolf Hitler was convinced that the Waffen-SS could undertake the most dangerous and difficult missions with impunity, and during the remainder of the war they would increasingly be relied upon by Hitler to deliver the victories he desired and thought possible. They in return tried to deliver the undeliverable without question of personal sacrifice.

Following the retaking of Kharkov, the situation stabilised somewhat on the southern sector of the Eastern Front. The Germans set about consolidating their positions. However, it soon became apparent that the Red Army had established a huge salient between Kharkov and Orel in the north. This salient extended into German territory and almost invited attack. Hitler was transfixed by this salient, and soon preparations were under way to eradicate it. The subsequent battle will be dealt with in the next chapter, but suffice to say that once again the Waffen-SS would be called upon to try and regain the German initiative on the Eastern Front. But the retaking of Kharkov had blinded Hitler to what was really happening on the Eastern Front: that despite his vaunted Waffen-SS, he was losing the war in the East, a fact that would be confirmed at Kursk.

Below: Tiger tank and an anti-aircraft SdKfz half-track of the Das Reich *Division. The achievements of I SS Panzer Corps had brought a false dawn of hope in the East. Hitler was convinced the mineral-rich Donetz basin had been permanently saved, and that his no-retreat policy had again been vindicated.*

CHAPTER 8

KURSK

The reputation and fighting abilities of the elite Waffen-SS divisions were extremely high in the summer of 1943. Hitler had no hesitation in committing them to his offensive designed to destroy the Kursk salient and regain the initiative in Russia. But the Russians were ready and waiting, and thus the scene was set for the greatest armoured battle in history, a battle in which the Waffen-SS would battle valiantly but in vain. Not even the supermen could achieve the near impossible and defeat the Red Army.

Left: Panzergrenadiers of the Das Reich *Division move forward during the Battle of Kursk in July 1943. The division was part of Hausser's II SS Panzer Corps.*

In the spring of 1943 Hitler saw that the Germans had to gain the initiative in the East by liquidating the Kursk salient. By doing so the German front would be dramatically reduced, and it would release troops to guard against the anticipated invasion of southern Europe by the Allies. It would have the added advantage of destroying up to 15 Soviet armies, and the German war effort would be greatly enhanced by the countless numbers of Soviet prisoners who would go into the bag and could be exploited as forced slave labour.

Field Marshal Erich von Manstein and General Heinz Guderian put forward a plan suggesting that the Soviets be allowed to go onto the offensive in order to over-extend themselves. Then the Germans would counterattack. Hitler was unimpressed, and insisted that the offensive be planned for and undertaken with all speed. It was to be codenamed Operation 'Citadel'. The

Chief of Staff of OKW (Armed Forces High Command), Field Marshal Keitel, expressed this view openly when he said, at one of the conferences in the Reich Chancellery: 'We must attack on political grounds.' Germany's military and political leaders also assumed that successes in the East would rattle the very foundations of the Allied coalition, causing it to disintegrate by increasing the dissatisfaction of the Russians at American and British delays in opening a second front on mainland Europe. Hitler wholeheartedly believed that 'the sooner a heavy new blow is struck at the Soviet Union the sooner the coalition between East and West will fall apart.'

After the plan had been considered at the highest level, Hitler issued an order on 15 April 1943 for an offensive in the Kursk salient. The order stated: 'This offensive is of decisive importance. It must end in swift and decisive success. On the

Above: In their makeshift shelters, these Waffen-SS soldiers relax before the opening of the Kursk Offensive. The assault was to demonstrate German superiority and reverse the disaster at Stalingrad. Hitler amassed 900,000 men, 2700 tanks and assault guns and 1800 aircraft for Operation 'Citadel'.

axis of the main blow the better formations, the best weapons, the better commanders and a large amount of ammunition must be used. Every commander, every private soldier, must be indoctrinated with awareness that the decisive importance of this offensive victory at Kursk will be a beacon for the whole world.'

According to the plan, the main blows at the Soviet forces were to be struck from south of Orel by the 9th Army of Army Group Centre, and from north of Kharkov by the 4th Panzer Army and operational group *Kempf* from Army Group South. By striking in the general direction of Kursk, the German High

Command reckoned to surround and destroy the forces of the Central and Voronezh Fronts defending the salient, to straighten the frontline, and in the event of success, to develop their offensive into the rear of the southwest front (Plan 'Panther'). Nor did they exclude the possibility of a subsequent strike to the northeast, to outflank Moscow and come out behind the whole of the Soviet forces in the centre.

Since such special importance was attached to the forthcoming battle, OKH (German Army High Command) reviewed and revised the operational plan several times, and Hitler stated more than once that 'there must be no failure'. Divisions which were to take part were rested and made up to full strength in men and equipment. Particular attention was paid to the Soviet defensive system in the salient and to the terrain.

The Germans were faced by Soviet forces of massive and power-ful might. General Rokossovsky commanded the Soviet Red Army on the Central Front, while General Vatutin commanded the Voronezh Font. Air Marshal Rudenko commanded the 2nd, and Air Marshal Krasovski the 16th Air Armies respectively, which were to supply airborne support. Eleven armies were positioned in the salient itself, while held in reserve was a further force commanded by Colonel-General Konev – the Steppe Front. Colonel-General Goryunov's 5th Air Army provided reserve air support. The Soviets could call on over 1,300,000 men, 3300 tanks, 20,000 artillery pieces and 2000 aircraft.

German strength at Kursk

In reply, Field Marshal Erich von Manstein, fielded his Army Group South. This comprised Panzer Group *Kempf*, commanded by its General Kempf, and was made up of XI Corps, commanded by General Raus, and the 106th and 320th Infantry Divisions; XLII Corps, commanded by General Mattenklott, comprising the 39th, 161st and 282nd Infantry Divisions; and III Panzer Corps, commanded by General Breith, comprising the 6th, 7th and 19th Panzer Divisions and 168th Infantry Division. The mighty 4th Panzer Army, commanded by Colonel-General Hoth, was the other portion of Army Group South. It comprised II SS Panzer Corps, led by SS-Obergruppenführer Paul 'Papa' Hausser, and comprised the 1st SS Panzer Division *Leibstandarte*, 2nd SS Panzer Division *Das Reich* and 3rd SS Panzer Division *Totenkopf*; XLVIII Panzer

Below: The first day of the offensive – 5 July 1943. Waffen-SS soldiers use a swastika flag as an aerial recognition symbol to stop them being strafed by Luftwaffe aircraft. But general progress was slow: the Russians had prepared their defences in depth, and planned to soak up the German assault.

Corps, commanded by General von Knobelsdorff, formed by the 3rd and 11th Panzer Divisions, 167th Infantry Division and Panzergrenadier Division *Grossdeutschland*; and LII Corps, commanded by General Ott and formed by the 57th, 255th and 332nd Infantry Divisions. General Dessloch's Air Fleet IV gave air support.

Field Marshal Günther von Kluge was a traditional Prussian officer showing considerable aptitude for his chosen profession. His command was Army Group Centre, whose forces consisted of Colonel-General Model's 9th Army, XLVI Panzer Corps under General Zorn, XLI Panzer Corps, commanded by General Harpe, XXIII Corps, commanded by General Freissner, and XLVII Panzer corps, commanded by General Lemelsen. Colonel-General Ritter von Greim's Air Fleet VI was to provide air support. The Germans could field all in all some 900,000 men, 2700 tanks and 10,000 artillery field pieces. Air cover would be supplied by 2000 Luftwaffe aircraft.

New panzers

Hausser's command formed under 10 per cent of the total German strength. Kharkov had been won using updated versions of the old Mk III and the newer Mk IV panzers, though a few of the more powerful Mk VI Tigers had seen service. Kursk would see more Tigers being used, but the Germans pinned their hopes on the Mk V Panther medium tank. The Ferdinand assault guns were also to be employed. The Soviet detection of the German

Left: A Waffen-SS soldier marches past a destroyed Russian T-34 at Kursk. SS losses were horrendous from the start. The Leibstandarte, *for example, lost 97 men killed and 522 wounded on the first day. The next day this had risen to 181 killed and 906 wounded – 10 per cent of the division's men killed in just two days.*

build-up was hardly an intelligence coup, so great were the movements required for the massive offensive.

Stalin's view was that the Soviet Red Army should take the offensive. His generals in the field thought differently: the German armies should be encouraged to attack, to be drawn into the salient. In attempting to smash through the Soviets' extensive defensive obstacles they would bleed themselves to death. Then would come the time to launch a savage counterattack. Stalin consented to the plan.

The Russian defences

The Russian front was reinforced with large numbers of guns, tanks and aircraft, the greatest concentration being made around the most likely axes of attack. As the Germans hoped to attain their objectives by massed use of tanks, the front commanders took special care over anti-tank defences, which were based on anti-tank strongpoints and areas and systems of minefields. Artillery reserves were allocated and trained in good time, as were mobile obstacle detachments. The strongpoints, as a rule, were allocated between three to five guns each, up to five anti-tank rifles, two to five mortars between a section, and a platoon of sappers and a section of submachine gunners. On the most vital axes, the anti-tank strongpoints had up to 12 guns each.

The depth of defence of the Central and Voronezh Fronts on the axes of probable attack reached 152-176km (95-110 miles). Adding the defence line of the Steppe Front and the defence line along the River Don came to 256-288km (160-180 miles) and comprised eight defence belts and lines. On the same front the engineers laid about 400,000 mines and ground bombs, and the average density of minefields along the Central and Voronezh Fronts was a staggering 2400 anti-tank and

2700 anti-personnel mines per mile of front.

The Soviets thought the German attack would come from the north. But this was a mistake. A Waffen-SS spearhead, formed from the *Leibstandarte, Das Reich* and *Totenkopf* Divisions' armoured formations, was to lead the German offensive on the southern side of the salient. The northern sector witnessed a massive artillery barrage, which started on 5 July at 0430 hours, heralding the beginning of the offensive. It had been launched by Army Group Centre to soften up the enemy positions. The Soviet defences had not suffered as badly as expected when the barrage stopped, and in the ensuing assault the Germans encountered Red Army units ready and willing for action.

A slow advance

Gun and heavy mortar fire was the Soviets' immediate response to the German troops, who tried to conceal themselves in the tall grass. The anti-personnel mines that had been laid now wrought havoc among the Germans. On the western flank the German push was beginning to bog down, with an advance of only a few kilometres having been achieved by the end of the first day. The 20th Panzer Division and the 6th Infantry Division, situated a little to the east, were having more success against the defences. The German panzer units' penetration into the salient was about 8km (five miles), a slightly better showing. Red Army aircraft were able to mount effective air attacks, despite the Luftwaffe having air superiority over the area, in which the Germans took heavy casualties in men and equipment.

The German armour suffered badly as well, not from the Soviet T-34s, which were knocked out by the Ferdinand tank destroyers and Tiger tanks, but from the dense Soviet minefields.

The town of Oboyan was the 4th Panzer Army's first objective, and initial progress was good. XLVIII Panzer Corps had the task of protecting the left flank of the assault. By the close of the first day, Panzergrenadier Division *Grossdeutschland*, in the company of the 3rd and 11th Panzer Divisions, was in the vicinity of Cherkasskoye and quickly overcame the first lines of defence around it. But this was at a cost: 36 of its new Panther tanks knocked out.

So as not to endanger the right flank of the Germans' advance, Hoth decided that the Soviet reserves had to be neutralised as a priority, rather than leaving them for later. With this purpose in mind, he ordered an attack to be launched in the direction of the northeast after the Soviet line had been penetrated. II SS Panzer Corps was given the mission

of eliminating the Soviets' reserves. In the German arsenal, II SS Panzer Corps was one of the strongest elements that could be unleashed on the enemy. It had an enormous spearhead of armour which comprised 200 self-propelled guns and 350 tanks. An integral Tiger unit was attached to each of the SS divisions.

The SS engineers had busied themselves and swept the first set of minefields aside, allowing easy passage through them for Hausser's troops, who began their assault at 0400 hours on 5 July.

The *Panzerkeil* (armoured wedge) was deployed to cut through the Soviet defences. The point was made up of Tiger tanks and flanked by Panthers. Standard Mk IV and Mk III Panzers with Sturmgeschützen, or assault guns, flanked the Panthers. By the close of the first day it had penetrated into the salient

by up to 19km (12 miles). Hausser's men had done well.

II SS Panzer Corps' right flank was guarded by the *Totenkopf* Division, its objective being the Soviet 52nd Guards Division, which it drove back back after heavy fighting. The Soviet 69th Army command post, which housed numerous high-ranking staff officers, was situated in the village of Yakovlevo, and was captured by the end of the first day.

The salient was penetrated up to 32km (20 miles) as the rapid advance of the division continued, with the main Belgorod-Oboyan road being crossed by the end of the

Below: Das Reich *panzergrenadiers at Kursk. The division ran into minefields near Beresov, but was able to effect a breach in the Russian line and open the road to Lutschki, allowing the division's armour to pour through.*

Left: German Army gunners pound Russian positions. On the first day the Leibstandarte and Das Reich Divisions penetrated along the line of the River Vorskla and the Totenkopf had broken through the Soviet 52nd Guards Rifle Division. But the Fourth Panzer Army had lost over 50 tanks.

was to be carried out by II Guards Tank Corps and had been ordered by General Vatutin. This powerful force would have smashed into the *Totenkopf* and II SS Panzer Corps' flanks. However, the Germans became aware of the move and before the Soviets could reach the *Totenkopf's* position they were subjected to a massed aerial attack which completely annihilated them.

More Soviet defence lines were attacked by the *Totenkopf* Division on 9 July, and under the savage onslaught the Soviet defences began to crumble within hours. On the following day the Waffen-SS soldiers reached the River Psel.

The extent of the advance was now causing deep concern to the Soviet commanders, who decided it was now time to commit the 5th Guards Tank Army and two tank brigades to crush the German armoured spearhead. They were thus moved from northeast of Prokhorovka, where they were being held in reserve.

On 5 July the *Leibstandarte*, which was positioned to the south of the *Totenkopf* Division, pushed

second day. But then Soviet resistance stiffened.

The following day, the *Totenkopf* plodded on with its slow but relentless progress, severing many important rail and road links with the salient being penetrated by a further 16km (10 miles). Luftwaffe Stukas, equipped with 37mm anti-tank cannon, rendered valuable assistance to the division.

The mission of covering II SS Panzer Corps' flank was given to the army's 167th Infantry Division, thus allowing the *Totenkopf* to concentrate on the advance. The SS soldiers spent 8 July waiting for their replacements to arrive.

The Russians decided to halt the Waffen-SS advance. The Germans were to be subjected to a counterattack that was to be launched from a spot northeast of Belgorod. This

Right: German artillery in action at Kursk. By the end of the first day headquarters of the Fourth Panzer Army was registering alarm. II SS and XLVIII Panzer Corps had broken through the first line of Russian defences but had fallen short of their objectives. The Russian plan of soaking up the pressure was working.

on with success. The first line of the Soviet defences was penetrated, but then the division's progress began to be stifled by increasing Soviet resistance. The *Leibstandarte*, on the first day of the offensive, suffered 522 wounded and 97 killed in action. This rose on the second day to 906 wounded and 181 killed, representing a 10 per cent casualty rate for the division in the space of 48 hours of combat. On the other hand, the Red Army was suffering casualty rates far in excess of those suffered by the Waffen-SS. Some units were to all intents and purposes wiped out.

From the Soviet pont of view, although the losses were appalling,

Above: German infantry and self-propelled anti-tank gun at Kursk. Ironically, German tactics during the battle were disappointing. By the morning of 8 July, mechanical failure had removed 76 per cent of Panthers from some German units, and the Panzerkeil *was not living up to expectations.*

they kept filling the gaps with replacements from what appeared to be a limitless manpower pool. The Germans did not have such manpower resources to call on, with trained reserves becoming scarcer. German Army units became bogged down on the flanks of Hausser's corps, but the Waffen-SS's advance continued despite their losses. But

by the end of the third day another problem presented itself: critical tank losses. Some 160 Panthers had been lost from its initial total of 200.

Soviet tanks were falling foul of the Tigers, which knocked them out before they could get close enough to be effective against the Tigers' massive armour. The Tiger was indeed a formidable opponent. Teething troubles of the mechanical type bedevilled the Panther, its newer companion. But it showed immense promise for the future. The Ferdinand had, through a design oversight, not been equipped with a machine gun for close-quarters defence. This small but critical oversight had left this monster, larger than the Tiger, with a defence blind spot. For once they had penetrated Soviet positions, they became very vulnerable to the satchel charges and Molotov cocktails of the Soviet 'tank destruction' teams. Their crews were left with little else but their personal weapons to defend themselves.

Wittmann – tank ace

The towns of Teterevino and Oboyan being the main objectives of the *Leibstandarte*, on 7 July it began to push forward in their direction again. SS-Untersturmführer Michael Wittmann proved his worth once more, knocking out seven enemy tanks of the Soviet 29th Anti-Tank Brigade with his Tiger. Wittmann and his crew had already knocked out eight enemy tanks on the first day of the offensive. It was not until early 1943 that he received his first Tiger tank on the Eastern Front. The secret of his success was patience, often waiting for his victim to come within very close range. By June 1944, he was accredited with 138 tanks and 132 vehicles destroyed. But it was at Kursk that he first entered the limelight, and by the end of the offensive he had destroyed 30 Russian tanks and 26 anti-tank guns.

Psyolknee was next in the sights of the Waffen-SS, who pushed inexorably towards it. However, between 50 and 60 T-34s were attempting to gain the rear of SS-Panzer Regiment 1. Finding himself faced with this formidable force, 20-year-old Tiger tank commander, SS-Oberscharführer Franz Staudegger, engaged the enemy. He knocked out 22 T-34s, while the remainder beat a hasty retreat. An immediate recommendation for the Knight's Cross of the Iron Cross was made for Staudegger, which was confirmed on 10 July 1943. A veritable graveyard of T-34s had been established in the area that surrounded Tetorevino, for 90 had been knocked out by the 2nd Battalion of Panzer Regiment 1, under the command of SS-Sturmbannführer Martin Gross, in just three hours, while SS-panzergrenadier 'tank destroying' units had accounted for a further 30 T-34s.

Stiff Russian resistance was being levelled at *Das Reich*, which at this time was positioned on the right flank of the *Leibstandarte*. Before the launch of the offensive, assault troops from the division had wormed their way into the enemy's first line of defences, which they were quickly able to immobilise. However, serious casualties were suffered by the division's second wave when it was caught in the Soviet barrage, which the initial German advance had brought on. The rain again played a major part, for the ground turned into a quagmire. The SS soldiers were also without any tank protection, the rain-soaked ground having delayed their heavy support vehicles.

The village of Beresov was the major objective on the first day of the offensive for *Das Reich*. With the support of Luftwaffe Stukas the division took the village. A ridge of high ground beyond the village was also taken as the division rattled on. Its objective achieved, the order to drive forward was given, so that the success could be exploited. There was an extensive belt of minefields at Bey and Beresov; when encountered, the momentum of the assault was halted. The Soviet lines were breached the following day, and *Das Reich*'s armour now flowed through the gap. In addition, the main road to Lutscki lay open.

The *Totenkopf* Division, leading II SS-Panzer Corps, carried on with its drive northwards, and to the west of Prokhorovka Soviet forces were pushed aside. The 5th Guards Tank Army was positioned a little way to the east of the town. This, the main reserve of the Soviets, was getting ready to spring its own offensive,

Below: Destroyed Russian T-34s near Prokhorovka, where 1000 tanks had clashed on 12 July. By nightfall the Germans had lost around 300 tanks, though more importantly their overall impetus had been halted. The clash at Prokhorovka effectively signalled the end of Operation 'Citadel'.

with the objective of bringing II SS-Panzer Corps to a standstill. However, the Russian preparations were rudely interrupted with the appearance of Hausser's command, which turned smartly eastwards, with the *Totenkopf* taking the left flank, the *Leibstandarte* the centre and *Das Reich* the left flank.

The Germans were held, just, to the west of Prokhorovka. The Soviets decided to implement a two-part plan. A force of two mechanised brigades, a mechanised guards corps, an armoured brigade and a guards rifle division were dispatched with the objective of intercepting III Panzer Corps (which was driving northwards) and halting or slowing it down, while the remaining force undertook an immediate attack on II SS Panzer Corps.

All Soviet positions that could be located were subjected to an enormous Luftwaffe bombing raid when the German attack started once more on 12 July. The *Panzerkeil* was again used by the Waffen-SS divisions. To complete the softening-up process, a tremendous artillery barrage was laid down on the Soviet positions.

The Russian charge

With the advantage of the sun at their backs, which was to dazzle their enemies, the Soviets broke cover and at full speed drove straight at the amazed Germans as the German artillery barrage ceased. The German gunners, very experienced in their art, gave a good account of themselves and many Soviet tanks were knocked out. The German tank lines were reached by a considerable number of Russian tanks, however, and battle commenced at virtually point-blank range. This favoured the Soviet T-34's lighter 76 mm gun. Tanks on both sides were taking direct hits and being blown to pieces. Often suicidal bravery was demonstrated

by many Soviet tank crews, who, once the ammunition was spent, deliberately rammed enemy tanks.

The *Totenkopf* Division, positioned on II SS Panzer Corps' left flank, was engaged by XXXI Guards Corps and XXIII Guards Corps, who halted the *Totenkopf*'s advance and forced it onto the defensive. Meanwhile, II Guard Tank corps was meting out stiff opposition to *Das Reich*.

Decision at Prokhorovka

The high point of the battle was reached by the afternoon, but the outcome hung by a thread and could have swung either way. The Soviet blocking force had achieved its objective and halted III Panzer Corps, which was battling to advance towards II SS Panzer Corps. This was a blow for Hausser.

In a desperate attempt to redress the situation and influence the result in its favour, the *Leibstandarte* regrouped. The very last vestments of the Soviet reserves were now committed to the fray as the Russians had successfully anticipated the Waffen-SS's move. By nightfall, with both sides utterly exhausted due to the fierce fighting that had raged all day, the battle was reduced to all but a handful of small individual skirmishes. Some 300 German tanks had been destroyed during the course of the day(when a German tank suffered a major mechanical defeat or was severely damaged it was to all intents and purposes destroyed, while the Soviets could recover and repair theirs). They took fearful casualties, but on the battlefield were in command of the situation. The German assault at Kursk had been halted.

Hitler decided to suspend Operation 'Citadel' on 13 July officially, although the fighting continued until 15 July. Nothing could come out of the battle, not even the smallest vestiges of a limited suc-

cess. Field Marshal von Manstein made the argument that the offensive could be seen to have some chance of limited success if it were relaunched, with the objectives scaled down to continue the pressure on the Soviets. The final nail in the coffin for Operation 'Citadel' was that Hitler was adamant that the *Leibstandarte*, *Das Reich* and *Totenkopf* Divisions be withdrawn from the Eastern Front. The Allied invasion of Sicily, which had begun on 10 July, and the consequences this might have in the Mediterranean theatre, pressed on Hitler's mind during the next three days, causing him to become increasingly concerned. The strengthening of the Italian Front, in his opinion, could only be achieved by his elite Waffen-SS divisions. The soft underbelly of Europe was potentially where Germany's greatest danger lay. Hitler gravely reduced the strength in the Kursk region to such a point where it was unlikely to sustain a Soviet counterattack. The offensive's territorial gains would all have to be sacrificed to the Soviets, and by 23 July had all indeed been retaken by them.

Battle casualties

The battle had inflicted resounding losses on both sides, losses which were never to be really overcome. The German losses were catastrophic in both men, which was estimated at around 100,000, and tanks. The Wehrmacht was never to recover from this disaster. The Eastern Front from now on was to drain the German forces through attrition. The initiative had been lost and would never be regained. Soviet losses were even more horrendous, to such an extent that they were concealed from the country until the collapse of the communist regime. They suffered over 250,000 killed and 600,000 wounded, and of their entire tank strength 60 per cent had

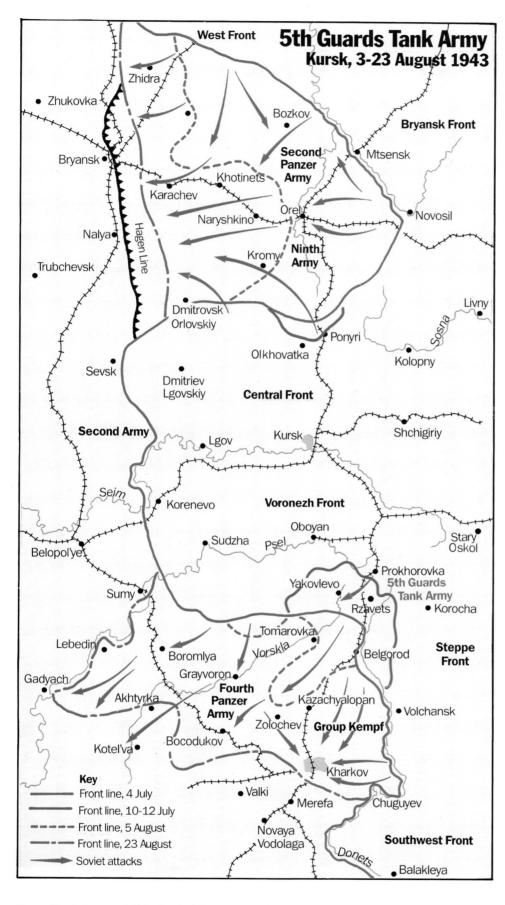

5th Guards Tank Army
Kursk, 3-23 August 1943

West Front

Zhidra

Zhukovka

Bozkov

Bryansk Front

Mtsensk

Second Panzer Army

Bryansk

Khotinets

Karachev

Orel

Novosil

Nalya

Naryshkino

Hagen Line

Trubchevsk

Kromy

Ninth Army

Dmitrovsk Orlovskiy

Livny

Sevsk

Ponyri

Sosna

Dmitriev Lgovskiy

Olkhovatka

Kolopny

Central Front

Second Army

Lgov

Kursk

Shchigiriy

Seim

Korenevo

Voronezh Front

Belopol'ye

Oboyan

Stary Oskol

Sudzha

Psel

Prokhorovka
5th Guards Tank Army

Sumy

Yakovlevo

Rzavets

Korocha

Lebedin

Tomarovka

Vorskla

Boromlya

Belgorod

Steppe Front

Gadyach

Grayvoron

Fourth Panzer Army

Kazachyalopan

Akhtyrka

Zolochev

Volchansk

Bocodukov

Group Kempf

Kotel'va

Kharkov

Key
—— Front line, 4 July
—— Front line, 10-12 July
--- Front line, 5 August
-·-· Front line, 23 August
→ Soviet attacks

Valki

Merefa

Chuguyev

Novaya Vodolaga

Southwest Front

Donets

Balakleya

Above: By 2 August 1943, the Red Army had recovered the ground lost in the German attack; the next day the Russian counteroffensive was launched after a massive artillery and air bombardment.

Belgorod fell on 6 August and Kharkov on 23 August. The Germans had lost the initiative on the Eastern Front, and by 27 August the Russians were poised to move into the Ukraine.

been destroyed. But for them the battle marked the turning point of their war. In Hitler's view once again the Waffen-SS had proved without doubt its superiority, which he believed was the result of Nazi ideological indoctrination. While army units on their flanks were being thrown back or at best held, his political warriors were even up to the last second advancing.

Before the Waffen-SS divisions could be transferred to the West, they were transported for a short period of rest to an area near Kharkov. On 25 July 1943, General Malinovsky ordered a counterattack to be launched against the German forces that were deployed in the Donetz basin. The German positions along the Mius river were attacked, and Field Marshal von Manstein's troops were overrun. On 30 July, the army's 16th and 23rd Panzer Divisions were moved south with all haste in the company of the *Totenkopf* and *Das Reich* Divisions. When they reached Stalino they were committed to battle. The front was stabilised, which involved three days of merciless butchery, and the Soviet push had been halted.

Waffen-SS fire brigades

The German situation was still very perilous, and they were soon to suffer two attacks delivered by three complete Soviet fronts around Belgorod and in the direction of Orel. The German lines had mammoth holes gouged into them by the advancing Red Army. To cover Field Marshal von Manstein's left flank once more, the *Totenkopf* and *Das Reich* Divisions were now hastily dispatched northwards. It was obvious that the situation on the Eastern Front was so volatile that not all the Waffen-SS units could be released from service, and it was only the *Leibstandarte* which was transported to Italy. For the Germans, the writing was on the wall.

CHAPTER 9

FRESH BLOOD

The disaster at Kursk meant the
Waffen-SS had to recruit fresh
divisions to stem the Red Army as
it headed west. This necessarily
meant an abandonment of the very
strict criteria set down by
Himmler with regard to SS
recruitment. This resulted in units
of differing quality wearing
Waffen-SS uniform, ranging from
the very good to others which were
militarily useless.

*Left: Latvian SS recruits in action against the Red Army in late
1943. The Waffen-SS raised two divisions in Latvia, the 15th and
19th Waffen-Grenadier Divisions, and both fought well.*

In general, the Waffen-SS units raised in western Europe performed well in battle. SS recruiting posters in these countries stressed the struggle against Bolshevism and the threat of international Jewry. Of the two themes, the crusade against communism had a stronger appeal for non-German recruits. The races who were of Nordic blood were particularly welcome in the Waffen-SS, including the Norwegians (above right), Danes (above centre) and the Dutch (above left and below). All these countries produced excellent units.

The failure of the Kursk Offensive had forced the Wehrmacht on the defensive in the East, and having sown the wind it was about to reap the whirlwind. Having successfully stopped what was to be the last great German offensive on the Eastern Front, the Red Army was poised to begin a massive attack all along the front to rip apart the 'Eastern Rampart', the deep defence lines upon which the German High Command hoped to hold the Russians indefinitely – a somewhat forlorn hope. The Russians, though, had other ideas.

Red Army offensives

The Red Army's main effort was directed in the southern sector, with five fronts – Central, Voronezh, Steppe, Southwest and South – advancing through the eastern Ukraine to reach and then cross the River Dnieper. Farther north, Kalinin and West Fronts were ordered to push forward around Smolensk to pin down large German forces which would be urgently needed elsewhere. STAVKA, the Soviet High Command, had mastered the art of balancing the actions of several fronts, thereby enabling great local superiority to be established in designated sectors. The Russians had also mastered the tactical problems of breaking through deep and strongly fortified defensive lines, and had a logistical system capable of re-supplying their armies during the advance to keep up the momentum. This was particularly important because the Germans laid waste towns and villages as they retreated.

Red Army tactics after Kursk concentrated on strategic and organisational flexibility, with heavy concentrations of artillery and a broad frontage of attack. When one or two breaches had been made in the German line, the main element of the attacking force was transferred into the breaches for maximum exploitation. The German Army, and Waffen-SS, response was to try to make the initial Soviet assault strike empty space by withdrawing units immediately prior to the Red Army attack. The tanks were held back to deal with Russian breakthroughs, the main German killing zones being covered by anti-tank weapons. German strongpoints were placed approximately 16km (10 miles) apart, which would hold the Russian attacks for 24 hours. The German troops would then fall back to the next defence line. Flank attacks could be launched against those Red Army units deployed to tackle each strongpoint. These tactics were very sound, but they could never do more than temporarily delay the Russian advance, albeit at heavy cost to Red Army units. The hope that the Red Army would, in Hitler's words, 'some day be exhausted' was totally unrealistic. During the battles to recapture Smolensk in August and September 1943, for example, the Red Army mustered over 20,000 artillery pieces and 1400 tanks, compared to the Germans' 8800 artillery pieces and 500 tanks.

The Waffen-SS on the defensive

What then of the Waffen-SS? Throughout the period 1941-43, the elite divisions of the Waffen-SS – the *Leibstandarte*, *Das Reich* and *Totenkopf* Divisions – had displayed qualities which the Führer regarded as being essential to victory: a refusal to yield ground, in the face of even the most determined opposition, and ruthless aggression in the attack. It was perhaps inevitable, therefore, that he should look to these units to save the situation in the East. Though the *Leibstandarte* was sent to Italy, *Das Reich* and the *Totenkopf*, and III Panzer Corps, were sent to Stalino to try to stem the Russian offensive in that sector. This they did in August 1943.

Their respite was brief, though, for on 3 August the Red Army attacked between Orel and Belgorod and ripped a huge hole in the German line. The *Totenkopf* and *Das Reich* Divisions were rushed to the Kharkov area to halt the collapse of Manstein's left flank. The Soviet Voronezh and Steppe Fronts – five armies with a superiority in tanks and guns of five to one over the Germans – attacked Belgorod and fell like a thunder clap upon the forces of Hoth's 4th Panzer Army and Army Detachment *Kempf*, commanded by General Werner Kempf. The Germans fell back in disarray, yielding Belgorod on 5 August. Soon there was a 48km- (30-mile-) wide gap in the German line between Hoth's and Kempf's forces, into which the Red Army commander, General Vatutin, poured troops. The Soviets bypassed Kharkov and then swung southwest towards Poltava. Their aim was to cut off Army Group South by taking the crossings over the Dnieper between Kiev and Zaporozhye.

Holding the Dnieper

The two Waffen-SS divisions were ordered by Manstein to halt the Russian attack towards the Dnieper and stop enemy armour from wheeling south and surrounding Kharkov, which was held by Army Detachment *Kempf*. *Das Reich* and the *Totenkopf* therefore dug in west of Kharkov, just south of Akhtyrka, and awaited the Red Army tanks. For seven days the Waffen-SS soldiers endured ferocious assaults, but they prevented the Russians reaching the Dnieper. Kempf's position in Kharkov was untenable, however, and he abandoned the city on 22 August to escape encirclement. For this he was sacked by Manstein on Hitler's orders, his army being redesignated the 8th Army and placed under the command of General Otto Wöhler.

Wöhler's task was to rebuild the German front west of Kharkov, and he was helped in this greatly by the efforts of *Das Reich* and the *Totenkopf*. Between 15 and 20 August, for example, *Totenkopf* led the encirclement and destruction of

Below: Recruits of the Freiwilligen Legion Niederlande *being congratulated after being awarded the Iron Cross. The unit was first committed to battle in Russia in January 1942, north of Lake Ilmen. It earned a special commendation for its performance. The legion was disbanded in May 1943.*

Vatutin's spearheads trying to encircle Kharkov from the west. The division then linked up with the still-intact 7th Panzer Division and thus re-established contact with the 4th Panzer Army. The two SS divisions then covered the retreat of the 8th Army, helping to avert a major German disaster.

Field Marshal Manstein correctly assessed that the Germans would have to retreat to the natural defence line of the Dnieper, which was grudgingly accepted by Hitler in mid-September. As the 4th Panzer and 8th Armies fell back to the river,

the *Das Reich* and *Totenkopf* Divisions covered the retreat. However, the Russians had recommenced their attacks, and both Waffen-SS divisions had a tough time of it preventing the Russians reaching the river as German vehicles and troops poured over the crossing points.

The SS soldiers were now very tired, but still there was to be no respite. A crisis had developed to the south, where Russian forces had

punched a hole in the German line between the right flank of Wöhler's 8th Army and the left wing of General Hube's 1st Panzer Army. Russian tanks raced south towards Krivoi Rog. The latter was the rail, supply and communications centre for Army Group South. It held vast quantities of supplies and ammunition, and its loss would have dealt a mortal blow to Army Group South.

By mid-October the Russians appeared to be within reach of the prize: they had smashed the 57th Army Corps and cut the rail link between Dnepropetrovsk and Krivoi Rog. Manstein desperately threw together a reserve force: Schörner's 40th Panzer Corps (which included the *Totenkopf* Division) and the remnants of the 9th and 11th Panzer Divisions and the 16th Panzergrenadier Division. The 40th Panzer Corps, spearheaded by the *Totenkopf*, counterattacked on 27 October from north of Krivoi Rog.

Above: Norwegian SS recruits being sworn in to serve the Führer. The first Norwegian SS unit was the Freiwilligen Legion Norwegen, *which had 1200 fully trained men by March 1942. Sent to northern Russia to try to halt the Russian advance, its members fought well. By August, however, it had been destroyed.*

The Russians were stopped in their tracks after a week of bitter fighting, losing 5000 prisoners and 500 tanks. They then pulled back, allowing the

evacuation of Krivoi Rog four months later, together with all the valuable supplies.

If the Waffen-SS divisions proved time after time their superior fighting qualities, there was a heavy price to pay: at Kursk, for example, Hausser's II SS Panzer Corps lost over 400 tanks. Such losses, in both equipment and personnel, would have quickly exhausted the Waffen-SS had it not have been for a decision taken by Hitler to substantially expand the organisation.

Enlargement of the Waffen-SS

First came the decision to upgrade the elite Waffen-SS units – the *Leibstandarte*, *Das Reich* and *Totenkopf* Divisions, plus the *Wiking* – to panzer divisions in appreciation of their worth. Then came his decision to increase the number of SS divisions of all types in recognition that the war would not be brought to a speedy end in the East. Finally, Hitler decided that such was the worth of the best SS divisions that they should be formed into a central reserve, which would intervene in critical situations, such as at Kharkov in early 1943.

The decision to increase the number of SS divisions was not taken lightly, for Hitler, up until the disaster at Stalingrad, still wanted to preserve the exclusivity of the SS. However, Stalingrad forced him to authorise the creation of new divisions. The first were the *Frundsberg* and *Hohenstaufen* Divisions, to raise which Himmler was forced to recruit native Germans for the first time. The third, the famed *Hitlerjugend* Division, was created from the 1926 class of the Hitler

Left: Danish SS recruits on parade. Freikorps Danmark *first fought on the Russian Front in May 1942, around Demyansk in support of the* Totenkopf *Division. It pushed back the enemy, but by August had suffered losses of 22 per cent.*

Youth. But there was a recruiting drive in parallel to the additions to the *Reichsdeutsch* (German nationals) formations, which was the creation of the Eastern SS. Though undoubtedly necessary, it effectively destroyed Himmler's guidelines of racial selection.

The strict racial criteria set down by Himmler for admission to the Waffen-SS could no longer be afforded: dedicated anti-communist soldiers were needed to replace battle casualties, and units were needed to safeguard rear areas against the partisans which had sprung everywhere in eastern Europe from 1942 onwards. Necessity resulted in a plethora of different national groups wearing Waffen-SS uniform: Estonians, Croats, Latvians, Ukrainians, Bosnians, Italians, Albanians, Russians, Azerbaijanis, Rumanians, Bulgarians, Tartars and Hungarians.

The Baltic SS recruits

The Baltic states were the first to offer recruits. The Latvians, for example, raised the 15th Waffen-Grenadier Division der SS, which first fought on the Eastern front in November 1943. It put up spirited resistance against relentless Russian assaults, being driven westwards in the face of the Red Army. The Estonians, too, provided a rich seam of recruitment for the SS to tap. The result was the 20th Waffen-Grenadier Division der SS, which fought bravely in 1944-45.

The Balts may have had some tenuous claim to be of Nordic blood, but not so the Balkan Muslims, Cossacks or Ukrainians. Indeed, according to Nazi ideology the Ukrainians were classed as subhumans. However, this fact was conveniently overlooked because of their vehement anti-communism (some 100,000 responding to a call to arms which Himmler issued in April 1943). The result was the 14th Waffen-Grenadier Division der SS,

which was first thrown into battle in mid-June 1944 near Brody in an attempt to halt the Soviet offensive in that sector. Of the 14,000 soldiers of the division which went into battle, only 3000 survived. However, such was the number of volunteers coming forward that the Germans were able to replenish its ranks.

The *Handschar* Division

Himmler had less success with the Balkan Muslim divisions he raised. The 13th Waffen-Gebirgs Division der SS *Handschar* was raised to battle partisans in Yugoslavia. Raised and then moved to France for training, the recruits took exception to attitudes displayed by their SS instructors, who viewed these soldiers drawn from a 'lesser race' with contempt. The recruits mutinied, the only SS unit to do so, and killed some of the German cadre staff. Himmler was outraged at the treatment meted out to the Muslims, but could do nothing but have the mutiny put down ruthlessly after German lives had been lost. The ringleaders were shot, though the division was not disbanded. Sent back to Yugoslavia, it committed many acts of brutality in its anti-partisan operations, notably against the Serb population.

As the situation on the Eastern Front worsened, Hitler came to depend even more on his SS divisions (though only those composed of German and 'Germanic' personnel). By the end of 1943, for example, seven of his 30 panzer divisions were Waffen-SS and five of his panzergrenadier divisions wore SS uniforms. The *Leibstandarte* made the journey between East and West no less than seven times, making a major assault on each arrival. In November 1943, for example, newly returned from Italy, it led an assault which restored the Dnieper Front.

In general, the massive expansion of the Waffen-SS from 1943 did not

ally be gauged by the amount of *Volksdeutsche* personnel it contained: the greater the ratio the less its combat efficiency.

Turning to the eastern European SS, they were, with one or two exceptions (the Baltic formations), militarily useless. This was not entirely their fault: they were originally envisaged as being irregular

lead to a commensurate rise in military prowess. The best units were those which had been established before then, with the *Volksdeutsche* (ethnic Germans) and eastern European formations varying in performance from excellent to very poor. The backbone of the Waffen-SS was its panzer divisions. Their leadership, training, equipment and morale was such that they postponed the ultimate defeat of the Third Reich.

Regarding the non-elite divisions of the Waffen-SS (if such a phrase is not contradictory), one is faced with a great many contrasts. Only the west Europeans – Danes, Dutch, Belgians, French and Norwegians – fought well, and they formed the numerically smallest group among

Above: Armoured vehicle of the Horst Wessel *Division. Recruited from* Hungarian Volksdeutsche *personnel, it was formed in 1943 and served on the Eastern Front. It fought until the end of the war, taking part in the retreat through Poland and Slovakia, finally ending the war east of Prague.*

Himmler's legions. *Volksdeutsche*, though theoretically a massive pool of recruits which Himmler could tap, proved disappointing. Theodor Eicke was particularly scathing about them, commenting that they used their alleged inability to understand the German language as an excuse to avoid dangerous or unpleasant assignments, even accusing them of cowardice. A Waffen-SS unit's military efficiency could usu-

units, and were equipped and trained to fight partisans and 'sub-versives'. They were brave enough against ill-equipped partisans and defenceless civilians, but their morale disintegrated when they came up against the Red Army units.

If the eastern European Waffen-SS formations were of highly dubious military value, units such as the Indian Legion were a complete joke. What was not a joke was the amount of weapons handed out to these units, which were badly needed elsewhere. In addition, they drained officers and NCOs from existing Waffen-SS divisions for training purposes. This was an indulgence the Third Reich could not afford in the last two years of the war.

Below: The Grand Mufti of Jerusalem with Azerbaijani SS volunteers. The recruitment of Eastern European races into the Waffen-SS made a mockery of the racial guidelines set down by Himmler regarding selection for the SS. Technically, for example, Ukrainians were classed as subhumans, though they too were accepted into the SS. The need for men who would fight the Russians was paramount.

CHAPTER 10

FIRE BRIGADES

Hitler committed his elite SS divisions to the campaigns in Italy and France in the hope that they could throw the enemy back into the sea. Though they were unable to do so, the Waffen-SS armoured divisions were the most formidable adversaries the British and Americans had to face, particularly in France, where the *Hitlerjugend* fought a fanatical campaign.

Left: A heavily camouflaged Hitlerjugend *StuG III in Normandy after the D-Day landings of 6 June 1944. The division was the first Waffen-SS unit to see action in Normandy.*

In the summer of 1943, a new Waffen-SS panzergrenadier division – *Reichsführer-SS* – was formed. It was built around a cadre of personnel from SS-Sturmbrigade *Reichsführer-SS*, which had been formed from soldiers of Himmler's personal escort unit. The commander of the new division was a former regimental commander in the *Totenkopf* Division: SS-Brigadeführer Max Simon. Formed in Corsica, it was transferred to the Italian mainland in October 1943 when the Allies took the islands of Sardinia and Corsica. When the Allies landed at Anzio, the division was still being trained, but elements had to be quickly rushed to the front. They remained in combat in the Anzio/Nettuno bridgehead until 9 March 1944.

Hitler, meanwhile, had become concerned with the possibility of his erstwhile Hungarian allies abandoning the Axis and joining the Russians. To pre-empt this he launched Operation 'Margarethe', and most of the remaining elements of the division were transferred to Hungary to seize power from Admiral Horthy's regime.

Reichsführer-SS in Italy

The Allied advance through Italy soon saw these units brought back, however, and the division was reunited in time to take on the British 8th Army, which drove it back past Siena and Pisa to Carrara. Engaged in heavy defensive fighting for the remainder of 1944, it became embroiled in anti-partisan actions, committing atrocities at Padule di Fucecchio and Sant'Anna di Stazzema. The division was involved in the massacre of civilians at Marzabotto in September.

Command of the division passed to SS-Oberführer Otto Baum in October 1944, another former *Totenkopf* regimental commander, and by January 1945 *Reichsführer-SS* was located in the far northeast

of Italy. Hitler then decided it would take part in the counterattack in the Lake Balaton area.

The only other major Waffen-SS unit to serve in Italy was the elite *Leibstandarte* Division, which had been transferred from the Eastern Front in July 1943, leaving its heavy equipment and armour in Russia. It took part in the disarming of Italian Army units after the overthrow of Mussolini's regime in September 1943, before returning to the Eastern Front in the autumn.

The Waffen-SS in Normandy

By June 1944, Hitler was aware that an Allied invasion attempt on the French coast was imminent. But where? When the Allied invasion forces waded ashore on the beaches of Normandy on 6 June, he refused to believe that this was the real invasion, insisting that it was a feint intended to draw his forces away from the Pas de Calais, where he believed the real invasion would take place. Thus by the time he was persuaded that it was not a feint, a fatal delay in striking back had already been suffered.

On the morning of 6 June, the *Leibstandarte* was situated near Bruges, Belgium, being part of the Armed Forces High Command's strategic reserve, which could not be committed to battle without Hitler's express orders. It actually left its location to head for the battlefield 11 days after the D-Day landings took place, being sent to the Caen area. The 12th SS Panzer Division *Hitlerjugend* was already in the area around Dreux, between Paris and Caen, and was the first Waffen-SS unit to see action in Normandy. In addition, the 17th SS Panzergrenadier Division *Götz von Berlichingen* was also committed to the Normandy battles within a week of the initial landings.

The *Das Reich* Division was initially situated in the south of France

near Toulouse, in anticipation of a possible Allied strike against southern France. It was ordered north to the invasion front soon after D-Day. As it did so it fought numerous actions against *Maquis* (Resistance) units, perpetrating a number of executions in Tulle and the atrocity at Oradour sur Glane. It reached the Normandy area by 10 July, and was moved into the line near Périers.

The *Hitlerjugend* attacks

The Allied forces at first maintained pressure at the eastern end of their bridgehead. One of the main objectives of General Bernard Montgomery's British 21st Army Group was the city of Caen. The first attempt to take the city was by direct assault on 6 and 7 June, supported by British and Canadian aircraft. The *Hitlerjugend* moved into positions around Caen on 7 June, and immediately set about forming an assault group to stop the advancing British forces. Under the command of SS-Standartenführer Kurt 'Panzer' Meyer, a battle group made up of three battalions of infantry and a considerable number of Panzer IV tanks, together with the army's 21st Panzer Division, took the offensive and the British advance was stopped in its tracks, with 30 Allied tanks being destroyed for the loss of just two panzers. The Allies were only temporarily brought to a halt, though, the Germans not being strong enough to force the British forces to retreat.

By 9 June, Major-General Fritz Bayerlein and his Panzer *Lehr* Division were also in position

Right: The Hitlerjugend *in Caen in June 1944. The battles in and around Normandy were a new experience for the Waffen-SS. Its men faced the so-called* Materialschlacht, *the unending lines of tanks, motorised infantry, artillery and air attacks which blunted even the most fanatical SS attacks.*

around Caen, though the heavy attacks by Allied fighter-bombers the division had to endure en route cost it over 200 vehicles of all types. Caen and the vital Carpiquet airfield were now defended by three strong panzer divisions.

General Montgomery now used the 51st (Highland) Division and the 7th Armoured Division to try and take Caen. The Scots were ordered to move east of the Orne river, while the 7th Armoured approached Caen from the northeast. In hard fighting lasting three days, however, the British made little or no progress in the face of determined resistance from the Germans, and the attack eventually ground to a halt.

On 10 June, the 7th Armoured Division attempted to force its way past the British 50th Division just to the west of Caen, but likewise made little progress. A gap in the German defences between Caumont and

Villers-Bocage had been spotted by the Allies, and the 7th Armoured Division immediately attempted to exploit this, British tanks entering Villers-Bocage on the morning of 13 June. At the same time, SS-Obersturmführer Michael Wittmann, commander of 2 Company, *schwere* (heavy) SS-Panzer Abteilung 101, was also entering the village with a force of four Tiger tanks and one Panzer IV. Wittmann himself encountered four British Cromwell tanks on entering the village, and in a brief firefight knocked out three while the fourth tried to outflank him, though it too fell victim to his deadly 88mm gun. Wittmann then rejoined the other Tigers and proceeded to attack an entire British armoured column. Driving along the side of the column, Wittmann knocked out a further 23 British tanks at point-blank range, plus a similar number of half-tracks and

other armoured vehicles. The shells of the British tanks just bounced off the Tigers' massive front armour plating, even at such close range.

By the time the four Tigers and the Panzer IV returned through the village, however, British tanks and a 6-pounder anti-tank gun were waiting for them. All five tanks were knocked out by shots through their thinner side armour, though their crews escaped. Wittmann's action had saved the flanks of the Panzer *Lehr* Division, and for his actions he was decorated with the Swords and Oakleaves to his Knight's Cross.

Below: Waffen-SS troops in action against British forces during Operation 'Goodwood' in July 1944. The tenacity of the Waffen-SS accounted for 200 British tanks destroyed and halted the operation. But such was the overwhelming Allied material and numerical superiority that the success could not be followed up.

By 14 June, the gap in the German lines had been sealed. Within a few days of the invasion, OKW ordered the 9th SS Panzer Division *Hohenstaufen* and the 10th SS Panzer Division *Frundsberg* from Poland to Normandy, though they didn't arrive until the end of June.

While this was going on, the 17th SS Panzergrenadier Division *Götz von Berlichingen* was fighting US troops south of Carentan. The town had been taken by American troops, who had broken out from the Omaha and Utah beaches. On 14 June, *Götz von Berlichingen*, understrength and short of its heavy weapons, plus some paratroopers, unsuccessfully attempted to evict the enemy, suffering heavy casualties in the process. The division remained in this sector for the remainder of June and July, struggling to hold back the Americans.

On reaching Normandy on 25 June, both *Hohenstaufen* and *Frundsberg* were committed to battle between Caen and Villers-Bocage. They ran straight into Montgomery's Operation 'Epsom', his attempt to take Caen. The British VIII Corps attacked along a 6km (4 mile) front between Carpiquet and Rauray. Once again he used some of his most experienced troops: the 15th (Scottish) Division, 11th Armoured Division and 43rd Wessex Division. The attack opened with massive artillery and naval bombardments, but the advance soon slowed as the German defenders fought tenaciously to stop the Allied advance. The Germans counterattacked on 27 June, though their assault was stopped by the 11th Armoured Division. The latter then crossed the Odon river and took the important Hill 112 on 29 June.

Above: Waffen-SS soldiers with a captured British infantryman in the Bocage. *By the end of July 1944 the Americans had broken out of the Normandy bridgehead, despite fanatical rearguard actions by the* Das Reich *and* Götz von Berlichingen *Divisions. Both divisions suffered heavily for their efforts.*

Hohenstaufen and *Frundsberg* were thrown into the attack, but the Waffen-SS soldiers were beaten back. Fortunately for the Germans, however, the Allies had expected an even heavier attack and had withdrawn the 11th Armoured Division back across the Odon, so Hill 112 fell back into German hands.

Meanwhile, American forces had resisted all attempts to throw them back into the sea and had broken out of their bridgehead to capture the port of Cherbourg. Fortunately for the Germans, their demolition engineers had been so efficient at destroying the port facilities when they retreated that barely 10 per cent of the anticipated level of supplies could be brought into the port by the Allies.

In Caen, the troops of the *Hitlerjugend* Division held on, despite heavy artillery, aerial and naval bombardment. The Waffen-SS troops were gradually forced to give way, however, and the British eventually reached the River Orne, which ran through the centre of Caen, but only at a heavy cost in casualties. The *Hitlerjugend* clung on to the remainder of the city. Then the *Leibstandarte* reached the front and took over the *Hitlerjugend*'s positions at Caen, allowing it to go into reserve north of Falaise.

Operation 'Goodwood'

On 18 July, the British launched Operation 'Goodwood', in which a massive tank force planned to advance along a corridor blasted through the German lines by a massed Allied bombing attack. Once again, however, a promising start soon stalled as the Germans quickly recovered from the three-hour bombardment, and tank and anti-tank fire soon began to exact its toll on Allied armour. Though the *Leibstandarte* was forced to give up most of Caen, the Allies lost over 400 tanks and the German defence line was still largely intact.

Earlier, on 25 July, the Americans had launched Operation 'Cobra', preceded by the usual massive aerial bombardment. The frenzied defence put up by *Götz von Berlichingen* resulted in it becoming dangerously exposed, and so it was forced to withdraw. The Germans were suffering badly from the attacks of Allied fighter-bombers, especially the German tanks attempting to negotiate the narrow, hedge-lined country roads of this *Bocage* country. Most

German movements had to be made in the dark, a factor which led to many fatal accidents.

On 26 July, the US 1st Infantry Division and 3rd Armored Division, attacking in the direction of Marigny, ran into heavy resistance from the badly battered *Das Reich* Division and the army's 353rd Infantry Division. After two days of bitter fighting the Germans had destroyed their plan of pushing on through to Coutances.

The Americans had more success on their left flank, with the 22nd Infantry Division meeting little more than sporadic resistance. The Americans exploited this lack of resistance to the full as their forces rolled back the Germans. Still fighting around Marigny, *Das Reich* was forced to rapidly reform its defences to guard against the new danger to its flanks. Despite its best efforts, however, the momentum of the American attack was impossible to halt, and Coutances fell on 28 July.

Avranches falls

On 29 July, a combined force from *Das Reich* and *Götz von Berlich-ingen* smashed through the US 67th Armored Regiment and the 41st Armored Infantry near St Denis le Gast, but the attack faded in the face of overwhelming Allied numerical superiority. To avoid encirclement the SS units were forced back towards Avranches, which fell to the US 4th Armored Division on 30 July.

On the same day, the British VIII Corps launched Operation 'Bluecoat', an assault in the direction of Vire. Although the 11th Armoured Division quickly seized the high ground around Le Bény Bocage, the drive to capture Vire was not prosecuted swiftly enough, and the Germans were able to reinforce their positions. A chance to roll up the German 7th Army had been missed, and Vire was able to hold out for a further seven days.

Above: Waffen-SS soldiers with captured British soldiers following the reduction of the Allied pocket at Arnhem in September 1944. Though the Hohenstaufen *and* Frundsberg *Divisions could muster only a few battle groups, the panzer units were still able to defeat the lightly armed paratroopers, though it took 10 days.*

The American battle plan now revolved around driving on beyond Mortain and Avranches to swing up to the Caumont-Fourgères line,

before sweeping south via Le Mans and Alençon. With Avranches in their hands, the German units in the Contentin peninsula were in great danger of being cut off. In an effort to split the American forces in two, Hitler ordered an offensive towards Avranches. Taking part were the 2nd Panzer Division, 116th Panzer Division and elements of the *Leibstandarte* and *Das Reich* Divisions. The attack was launched late on 6 August, with *Das Reich*

soon taking Mortain and the high ground around St Hilaire. The 2nd Panzer Division also made good progress, before being slowed down by determined US resistance. However, the 116th Panzer Division made almost no progress from the start, and the whole German offensive soon began to falter.

II Canadian Corps had, meanwhile, begun an assault along the Caen-Falaise road as part of Operation 'Totalize'. As the Ameri-

can XV Corps moved towards Argentan, the Canadians in the north tried to link up with it. The Germans again faced the danger of being encircled. Hitler therefore approved a withdrawal from the Mortain area on 11 August, with the *Leibstandarte* and 116th Panzer Divisions concentrating their battered remnants around Carrouges for a counterattack against the Americans. Elements of the 116th Panzer Divisions did temporarily halt the US advance near Mortrée, but it was a brief respite. The *Leibstandarte* and 2nd Panzer Division arrived in Argentan on 13 August, but had to cancel any thoughts of a counterattack because the situation was deteriorating rapidly. Meanwhile, *Frundsberg* was battling to hold back the Americans around Domfront. It soon became clear that only a retreat through the Falaise-Argentan gap would save the German forces in Normandy.

The Falaise Gap

Withdrawal towards the River Orne began on 16 August. Initial progress was good, but by 17 August the 4th Canadian and 1st Polish Armoured Divisions were pushing southwards, while units of General Patton's US 3rd Army struck north. In between was the *Hitlerjugend* Division, desperately battling to hold open the gap. *Das Reich* and *Hohenstaufen*, which had both passed through the gap earlier, turned about and launched counterattacks against the Allies in a desperate attempt to gain time. German vehicles still inside the pocket became a prime target for Allied fighter-bombers, resulting in heavy German losses.

British and American units finally met at Chambois on the night of 19 August and the gap was closed. The line, though continuous, was not watertight, and some German units did manage to escape, one of them being *Götz von Berlichingen*. By the afternoon of 21 August 1944, the battle for the Falaise Pocket was over.

What was left of the *Leibstandarte* was withdrawn to Aachen for rest and refitting, while *Das Reich* was withdrawn into Germany. The *Hitlerjugend* retreated to the area east of the Maas, and *Götz von Berlichingen* was deployed to the Metz area. *Hohenstaufen* and *Frundsberg* were sent to Holland to refit, in a quiet place where they would not be disturbed: Arnhem.

After the defeat of the German forces in Normandy, Bernard Montgomery, now a field marshal, wanted permission to push through Holland, though General Patton insisted that an attack through the Siegfried Line defences via Lorraine was the best route into Germany. Montgomery eventually won, persuading Eisenhower, the Allied supreme commander to approve a combined ground and airborne assault through Holland codenamed 'Market Garden'. This plan called for the capture of the bridges at Eindhoven and Nijmegen by American airborne troops, while the British would capture the furthest bridge at Arnhem. While this was going on, the British XXX Corps, under Lieutenant-General Brian Horrocks, would push through from Belgium and link up with the airborne assault troops.

The Waffen-SS at Arnhem

The airborne assault was launched on 17 September 1944, and as the Allied airborne aircraft unloaded their paratroopers, intelligence reached the commander of Army Group B, Field Marshal Walter Model, who immediately placed his forces, which included II SS Panzer Corps under SS-Obergruppenführer Willi Bittrich, on alert. Actually the SS corps was made up of the survivors of the *Frundsberg* and *Hohenstaufen* Divisions who escaped from Normandy. However, they were good troops and would prove worthy opponents of the British 1st Airborne Division which landed at Arnhem.

While the American soldiers of the 82nd and 101st Airborne Divisions quickly consolidated their positions and took the bridge and town of Eindhoven and reached Nijmegen on schedule, they began to encounter strong German resistance. At Arnhem things were even worse. Because of unfavourable ter-

rain, the troops had been landed as far as 13km (eight miles) from the city itself, and were soon to find themselves fighting Waffen-SS panzer soldiers. Bittrich immediately sent *Hohenstaufen* to halt the British airborne troops at Arnhem, while a battle group from *Frundsberg* was sent to Nijmegen to help block the advance of XXX Corps. In addition to these two units, other SS troops took part in the Arnhem battles, including the staff of the SS-Unterführerschule at Wolfheze, 400 troops from the 16th SS-Stammbataillon and some Dutch SS police.

The Waffen-SS stops XXX Corps

By the end of 17 September, Lieutenant-Colonel John Frost's 2nd Parachute Battalion had forced its way on to the northern end of the Arnhem bridge and had taken the surrounding houses. A few troops from the 1st Parachute Brigade had arrived during the night to bring Frost's formation up to a strength of 600 men. The British were by no means strong enough to take the whole bridge, as at the other end were Waffen-SS panzergrenadiers.

On the morning of 19 September, an attempt by the majority of 1 Para Brigade to force its way to the bridge was stopped by the Germans, including SS Battlegroup *Spindler*. To the west of the city, Polish glider-borne troops landed in between the 4th Airborne Brigade and SS Battlegroup *Krafft* and were annihilated. At the bridge, meanwhile Frost was down to a mere 250 men, but he was still able to repulse all German attacks against him. All the while, Lieutenant-General Horrocks' XXX Corps was struggling to force its way through to Arnhem in the face of stiff German resistance and heavy aerial strafing.

At midday on 21 September, SS Battlegroup *Knaust*, commanded by Oberst Hans-Peter Knaust, forced its way over the bridge at Arnhem,

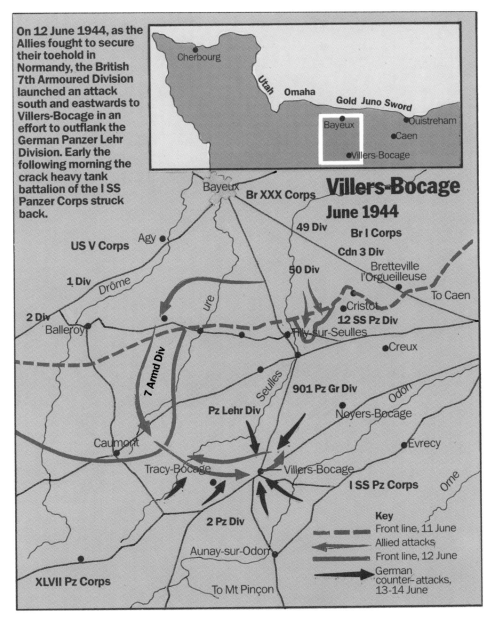

On 12 June 1944, as the Allies fought to secure their toehold in Normandy, the British 7th Armoured Division launched an attack south and eastwards to Villers-Bocage in an effort to outflank the German Panzer Lehr Division. Early the following morning the crack heavy tank battalion of the I SS Panzer Corps struck back.

Villers-Bocage
June 1944

Key
Front line, 11 June
Allied attacks
Front line, 12 June
German counter-attacks, 13-14 June

Left: On 12 June 1944, SS-Obersturmführer Michael Wittmann, leading a small force of tanks, including his own Tiger, destroyed 27 Allied tanks and over 20 half-tracks and other vehicles at Villers Bocage. In the process he had single-handedly eliminated the British 22nd Armoured Division.

ending Frost's heroic efforts. Knaust had no time to celebrate his victory, as he was immediately sent south to block those Allied troops which had finally forced their way over the Nijmegen bridge. Only 17km (11 miles) separated XXX Corps from the remnants of the British force around Arnhem, which was being squeezed into a small pocket at Oosterbeek. This was close enough for XXX Corps to provide artillery support for the beleaguered airborne troops, commanded by Major-General Robert Urquhart.

On 21 September, Major-General Stanislaw Sosabowski landed at Driel with the 1st Polish Parachute Brigade, to find himself faced with a

German force, which had by now decidedly gained the upper hand. Facing his men was a composite force under SS-Obersturmbannführer Harzer, made up of a mixture of naval, Luftwaffe, army and coastal defence troops, as well as some Dutch SS.

Both sides were by now totally exhausted after the vicious fighting, but it was the Germans who received the first major reinforcements in the shape of schwere Panzer Abteilung 506, complete with the powerful Panzer VI King Tiger tanks, against which the light anti-tank weapons of the British airborne soldiers were all but useless. Two companies of Tigers were

despatched to *Frundsberg* to help it hold back the advance of XXX Corps, while the third was turned against the weary survivors in the Oosterbeek area. The remnants of the British force were ordered to withdraw on the night of 25/26 September, and the survivors withdrew over the Lower Rhine at Oosterbeek and headed south.

Plans for the Ardennes Offensive

Though the victory at Arnhem gave a much-needed boost to German morale, Hitler had become obsessed with a grander plan to regain the military initiative in the West. Codenamed 'Wacht am Rhein', it was intended as a three-pronged attack towards Antwerp. The spearhead of the offensive was to be the 6th Panzer Army under the command of SS-Oberstgruppenführer 'Sepp' Dietrich, which was to attack through the Ardennes forests, get across the River Meuse between Liège and Huy, and then drive on towards Antwerp.

General Hasso von Manteuffel, commander of the 5th Panzer Army, was to strike northwest along Dietrich's southern flank, cross the Meuse between Namur and Dinant and head for Brussels. The 7th Army, under General Erich Brandenberger, meanwhile, was to drive for the Meuse on the southern flank. The capture intact of the bridges over the Meuse was vital to the plan, after which the drive on Antwerp would be supported by the 15th Army under General Student, in Holland. This, it was hoped, would trap the American 1st and 9th

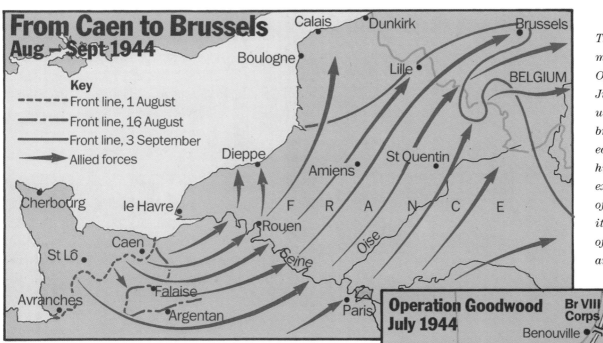

From Caen to Brussels
Aug – Sept 1944

Key
- – – – – Front line, 1 August
- – · – · – Front line, 16 August
- ——— Front line, 3 September
- ——▶ Allied forces

Though the Waffen-SS managed to blunt Operation 'Goodwood' in July 1944 (below), it was unable to stop the Allies breaking out and sweeping east (left). Losses were high. The Hitlerjugend, for example, lost 80 per cent of its troops, 80 per cent of its tanks, and 70 per cent of its armoured vehicles and artillery.

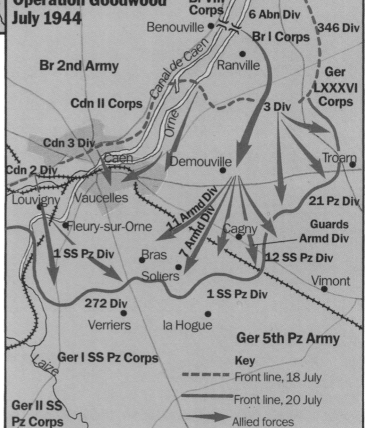

Operation Goodwood July 1944

Key
- – – – – Front line, 18 July
- ——— Front line, 20 July
- ——▶ Allied forces

Armies, British 2nd Army and Canadian 1st Army.

The armoured element of Dietrich's 6th Panzer Army consisted of I SS Panzer Corps, whose principal components were the 1st SS Panzer Division *Leibstandarte* and the 12th SS Panzer Division *Hitlerjugend*. In reserve was II SS Panzer Corps, made up of the 2nd SS Panzer Division *Das Reich* and the 9th SS Panzer Division *Hohenstaufen*. The infantry divisions comprised the 12th, 272nd, 277th and 326th Volksgrenadier Divisions and the 3rd Fallschirm Division.

In order to capture intact the bridges over the Meuse a special unit was created: Panzerbrigade 150, commanded by SS-Sturmbannführer Otto Skorzeny. It was made up of English-speaking volunteers, who were kitted out in American uniforms and issued with American weapons and vehicles. They were sent into action ahead of the main German strike force to mingle with the retreating Americans and spread confusion along the way, misdirecting the fleeing troops and sowing the seeds of panic.

The spearhead of the 6th Panzer Army was to be formed by I SS Panzer Corps, which was ordered to punch through the American lines between Hollerath and Krewinkel and drive through to the Liège-Huy sector, with the *Hitlerjugend* on the right flank and the *Leibstandarte* on the left. However, as the route was unsuitable for cross-country movement, it was vital for the Germans to get control of the roads. They were well aware of the difficulties even a small number of determined defenders could cause in such terrain, and so the point of I SS Panzer Corps' attack was given to a powerful assault group led by a man who had proved himself in combat on the Eastern Front: SS-Obersturmbannführer Joachim Peiper.

The Ardennes Offensive began on the morning of 16 December 1944 with, a massive artillery barrage. The 12th Volksgrenadier Division advanced through the weak American defences around Losheim and made a breach in the enemy's line, which Battlegroup *Peiper* was quick to exploit. Two companies of Panzer IV tanks led, followed by two companies of Panzer V Panther medium tanks and accompanying half-tracks containing infantry. Artillery and combat pioneers followed, with the massive King Tiger tanks of schwere (heavy) SS-Panzer Abteilung 501 bringing up the rear.

Progress along the congested roads was slow, though, with Battlegroup *Peiper* becoming entangled with slower-moving units, such as the 12th Volksgrenadier Division and paratrooper elements. By late evening Peiper's men were approaching Losheim, where the 3rd Fallschirm Division had forced a breach in the enemy lines to the south of the village, and Peiper immediately rushed his unit through the gap and raced on towards Lanzerath, linking up with Fallschirmjäger Regiment 9. He pressed on through the night, and just before dawn on 17 December the Germans found themselves amidst retreating American units moving through Honsfeld. The soldiers were taken completely by surprise by the appearance of Waffen-SS in their midst, and surrendered after offering token resistance.

Battlegroup *Peiper* slows

By now running low on fuel, Peiper diverted towards Büllingen and captured an American fuel dump there, which allowed his force to replenish its fuel stocks, before pressing on to capture Schoppen, Ondenval and Thirimont by the middle of the day. The battlegroup's line of advance now led it towards Ligneuville, where it met some resistance from American tanks before taking the town. Peiper remained in the town to confer with the commander of the *Leibstandarte*, SS-Oberführer Wilhelm Mohnke, while his men continued on towards Trois Ponts

and Beaumont. However, without its leader the Waffen-SS force became cautious when it met resistance at Stavelot, its lead vehicles having come under fire from US troops. The Germans drew back for the night and prepared to attack again in the morning.

Peiper takes Stavelot

By daybreak Peiper had returned to his unit, and the town was stormed after a heavy artillery barrage. The bridge at Stavelot was then captured intact, and by mid-morning the battlegroup was leaving the town behind and pressing on towards Trois Ponts (it acquired its name from the three bridges over the River Amblève and the Salm at this location). The Americans, however, succeeded in blowing the bridge over the Amblève, and all subsequent attempts by the SS soldiers to ford the river were unsuccessful. Peiper was therefore forced to turn north, and found an alternative bridge at Cheneux, near Stoumont.

Despite being delayed by Allied fighter-bombers, Peiper had now only two bridges between him and his primary objective: Huy. One of them, at Neuf Moulin, was blown as Peiper's troops approached. Though two alternative bridges were found nearby, both were too small to support his heavy

Right: Tank ace Michael Wittmann, here in the uniform of an SS-Obersturmführer. He destroyed a total of 138 enemy tanks and 132 anti-tank guns during a two-year career. Offered the post of a tutor at a panzer warfare school, he turned it down. Going back into action, he was killed in battle south of Caen on 8 August 1944.

vehicles (he had no heavy bridging equipment). Leaving some troops behind to guard the bridge at Cheneux, Battlegroup *Peiper* withdrew into woods for the night.

Things then started to go wrong. The Americans retook Stavelot, and on 19 December Peiper had to fight a two-hour pitched battle with the Americans before he could take Stoumont. On 21 December, Peiper decided to concentrate his forces around La Gleize and try to hold the bridge at Cheneux, but the Germans were driven out. Two days later, out of fuel and low on ammunition, Peiper and his remaining 1000 men set out for the German lines.

The other SS units fared no better. The *Hitlerjugend*, for example, struggled against American defensive positions. It was then directed south to clear the Büllingen-Malmédy road. Heavy losses were incurred, especially during the fighting for Büfenbach, and the division was withdrawn on 23 December 1944 to regroup.

Das Reich had been waiting in its assembly area near Jünkerath for orders to follow *Hohenstaufen* into action when it was attached temporarily to Manteuffel's 5th Panzer Army. It fought in the St Vith salient on 22 December and captured the vital crossroads at Baraque de Fraiture the next day. On the 24th, Manhay was taken, but further progress was stopped by American resistance, and by the 27th, Manhay had been lost again.

The *Hitlerjugend, Das Reich* and *Hohenstaufen* Divisions were all involved in an attack in the Manhay sector on 27 December, but failed to penetrate the American lines. The whole offensive was now bogged down, as Allied numerical superiority and air power, combined with German supply problems, began to take their toll. All hopes of reaching Antwerp, the original objective, were forgotten. Hitler now came up with a new plan designed to draw Allied units away from the Ardennes sector and give some relief to his tired assault forces. This new offensive, Operation 'Nordwind', was launched on 1 January 1945. Aimed at the weak American forces in the province of Alsace, the Waffen-SS units taking part included the 17th SS Panzergrenadier Division *Götz von Berlichingen* and the 6th SS

Below: The Ardennes Offensive was the last major German assault in the West. On the morning of 16 December 1944, 20 German divisions moved forward on a 112km (70-mile) front between Monschau and Echternach. But initial progress was poor.

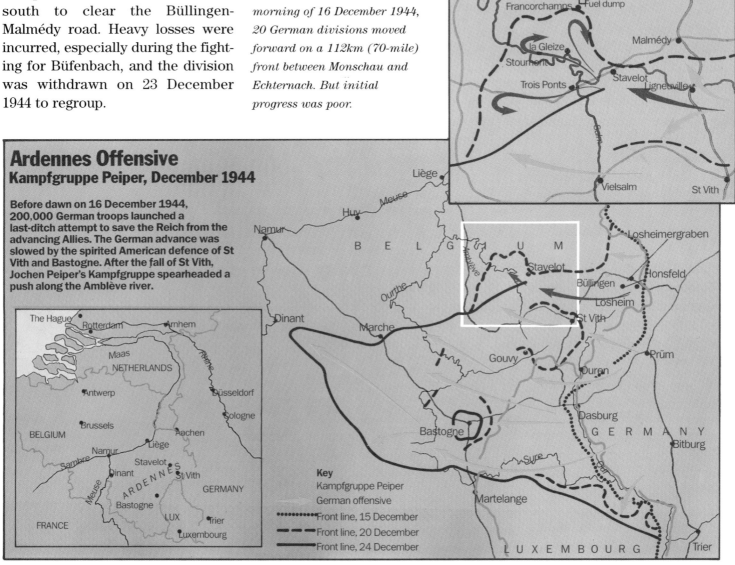

The Amblève valley

Ardennes Offensive
Kampfgruppe Peiper, December 1944

Before dawn on 16 December 1944, 200,000 German troops launched a last-ditch attempt to save the Reich from the advancing Allies. The German advance was slowed by the spirited American defence of St Vith and Bastogne. After the fall of St Vith, Jochen Peiper's Kampfgruppe spearheaded a push along the Amblève river.

Key
Kampfgruppe Peiper
German offensive
•••••••• Front line, 15 December
– – – Front line, 20 December
—— Front line, 24 December

Above: The fate of many Germans who took part in the Ardennes Offensive. Hitler's gamble failed, and by mid-January 1945 the Allies estimated that the Germans had suffered 120,000 casualties, lost 600 tanks and assault guns, 1620 aircraft and 13,000 vehicles. Such losses could not be replaced.

Gebirgs Division *Nord*, recently evacuated from the far north of the Eastern Front. Although initial successes were achieved and several hundred US prisoners were taken, the attack foundered within a few days. A fresh assault by *Frundsberg*, aimed at Strasbourg, also quickly ran out of steam, and no further German gains in Alsace were made.

In the Ardennes, meanwhile, the *Hitlerjugend*, *Leibstandarte* and *Hohenstaufen* Divisions were all heavily involved in the attempt to take Bastogne before it could be relieved by Patton's 3rd Army, but by 24 January 1945 the situation in

Hungary had deteriorated so seriously that all four divisions were withdrawn and committed to the Eastern Front.

By 10 February 1945, the last German units were back over the River Rhine. Germany's precious reserves had been squandered in the Ardennes, and the remaining Waffen-SS units on the Western Front could do little more than undertake a rearguard action as the Western Allies pushed into the Reich. By early 1945, not even the elite Waffen-SS could reverse the dire military situation faced by Nazi Germany on all fronts.

Right: Carrying an MG42 machine gun, this soldier of the Hitlerjugend *Division wears an Italian camouflage uniform – a consequence of the general uniform shortages in Germany in 1944. By August 1944, because of its great courage in Normandy, the division had only 300 men, 10 tanks and no artillery.*

CHAPTER 11

THE BLACK GUARD CRUMBLES

The floodgates in the East burst open in 1944, and the Waffen-SS was caught in the deluge. Despite its almost superhuman efforts, it could not prevent the Russians reaching the borders of the Third Reich itself.

Left: Waffen-SS anti-tank gunners await the next Russian attack. By mid-1943 the Red Army had a numerical superiority of four to one over the Germans along the whole Eastern Front.

The latter half of 1943 was a time of crises for German forces in the East, which were often only saved from turning into catastrophes by the intervention of Waffen-SS units. By mid-August, for example, a 55km-(34-mile-) wide gap had opened up in the German lines west of Kursk, and Red Army units began to pour through it, threatening Kharkov once again. The *Wiking, Das Reich* and *Totenkopf* Divisions were all thrown into battle to prevent the loss of the city (though weakened by the Kursk disaster, *Das Reich* had received all of the *Leibstandarte's* armour before the latter had been

Right: A well-wrapped Totenkopf *Division soldier equipped to survive the Russian winter. The division was in almost continuous combat from mid-1943 to the end of the war, as Hitler and his generals desperately tried to stop the Russian advance. Despite its best effort, the* Totenkopf *could do nothing to alter the strategic situation.*

transferred to Italy, making it a formidable fighting force). In a reversal of the German capture of Kharkov in March, it was now the Red Army's turn to launch a massive pincer attack, with the 53rd Army driving in from the north and the 57th Army from the south (the 5th Guards Tank

Army was to apply the hammer blow). The Russian attack was not quite as effective as the German one, though. The Soviets ran into strong defences, and on just one day of fighting Waffen-SS anti-tank gunners knocked out over 180 Russian tanks (Russian tactics still tended to be somewhat unsophisticated). However, such was the strength of the Red Army that it could only be delayed, and Manstein, fearing encirclement, ordered the city abandoned on 22 August.

Left: 'If you answer the call of the Waffen-SS and volunteer to join the great front of SS divisions, you will belong to a corps which from the very beginning has been associated with outstanding achievement.' So ran the SS's recruiting pitch. It might also have added that there was a good chance of the recruit ending up dead.

Over the next few weeks the *Wiking*, *Das Reich* and *Totenkopf* Divisions achieved some outstanding successes in small-scale combats with armoured units of the Red Army. On 12 September, for example, *Das Reich* destroyed 78 enemy tanks in one engagement. However, the Russians seemed to have little problem in replacing such losses, whereas the hard-pressed Waffen-SS units found it increasingly difficult to maintain their own strength.

Hitler agreed to von Manstein's Army Group South withdrawing to the line of Melitopol and the River Dnieper, thus retaining the strategically important western Ukraine in German hands. The withdrawal, undertaken in the face of Soviet pressure, was completed by 30 September. By that time a total of 68 German divisions – 1,250,000 men and over 2000 tanks of Army Group South – was tasked with holding the river line at all costs. Opposing them, however, the Red Army fielded a force almost twice as strong and better equipped.

The retreat to the Dnieper

In late August, Soviet forces began to advance and the Waffen-SS took part in a spirited withdrawal towards the River Dnieper. Yelnya fell to the Red Army after two days of bitter fighting, but the Russians were made to fight for every metre of ground and had to pause within a week to regroup. Then the offensive continued, the Russians capturing Bryansk, Smolensk and Roslavl in quick succession. By 2 October the Germans had been driven 240km (150 miles) westwards.

In November 1943, the *Leibstandarte* was released from duty in Italy and was sent back to the Eastern Front. It was allocated to XLVIII Panzer Corps of the Fourth Panzer Army, deployed to the south of Kiev in the Ukraine. Despite the sterling efforts of the *Das Reich*

Division, which was operating near Kiev, the city fell to the Russians on 7 November. The *Leibstandarte* did have some localised successes against Red Army units in the Kiev sector, but again these represented only delaying actions.

Between mid-November and the end of the year, both the *Leibstandarte* and *Das Reich* Divisions took part in a number of counterattacks as part of XLVIII Panzer Corps, but the weakness of the German forces was plain for all to see. At Korosten, for example, the *Leibstandarte*, together with the 1st and 7th Panzer Divisions, attempted to encircle a number of Red Army units. This was achieved, but the German units were spread so thinly that they could not maintain their positions, and soon the Germans were themselves fighting desperately to avoid encirclement. At Brusilov, XXIV Panzer Corps, to which *Das Reich* had been allocated, was simply overwhelmed in bitter hand-to-hand fighting by massive Russian forces. The remnants of the division, together with the *Leibstandarte*, retreated towards Zhitomir. The *Leibstandarte* was then deployed to Berdichev, where it linked up with the 1st Panzer Division and succeeded in halting the Red Army advance in that sector, but only for a short time.

The *Totenkopf* on the Dnieper

The remaining division of II SS Panzer Corps, the *Totenkopf*, had assumed the role of a fire brigade, continuously rushing from one threatened sector to another. In November and early December 1943, for example, it served with Hube's First Panzer Army, which was attempting to hold Krivoi Rog and the defensive positions on the Dnieper. On 12 December, together with the 11th and 13th Panzer Divisions, it halted the Soviet advance in that sector.

On 24 December 1943, the Russian forces in the southern sector of the front continued their push westwards from their positions around Kiev. Zhitomir was quickly recaptured, and only a determined effort by Manstein's forces slowed the enemy advance, though not before some German units had already been pushed back by as much as 160km (100 miles), being badly mauled in the process.

Cherkassy is isolated

At this juncture the Soviets attempted to smash German forces around Kirovgrad. They captured the town on 8 January 1944, but found German resistance stronger than expected. Some 11 German divisions were involved, including *Wiking* and the SS Sturmbrigade *Wallonie*, the Belgian Walloon volunteer unit recently transferred to Waffen-SS control. These strong German units posed a serious threat to Koniev's northern flank and Vatutin's southern flank. This German-held salient would have to be eradicated to ensure the success of the Soviet attack. Koniev renewed his attack on 25 January, and by the 29th 60,000 German troops had been encircled near Cherkassy. A sudden thaw turned the terrain into a boggy morass, making movement all but impossible. The airfield within the pocket, which the Luftwaffe was using to resupply the isolated divisions, suddenly became unusable. Constant pressure from the Russians saw the salient shrink rapidly, until it measured only 65 square kilometres (40 square miles) by 9 February.

Like on earlier occasions, Hitler refused to entertain any talk of a breakout by the encircled units, insisting that only an offensive by Manstein's forces to relieve them was a viable option. The Red Army, however, had thrown a ring of 35 divisions around the salient, and any

escape attempt by the trapped forces looked unlikely to succeed. Fortunately, Hitler was persuaded to allow the encircled units to attempt a breakout. The only armoured unit in the pocket, the 5th SS Panzer Division *Wiking*, commanded by SS-Obergruppenführer Herbert Otto Gille, would cover the flanks, while SS Sturmbrigade *Wallonie* formed the rearguard.

Breakout from Cherkassy

On the night of 16 February, the breakout began. Movement over the waterlogged terrain was difficult, and once the Russians became aware of what was happening a heavy barrage of artillery and rocket fire was laid down on the fleeing Germans. The wounded had to be left behind, as did most of the artillery and other heavy equipment. SS Sturmbrigade *Wallonie* suffered dreadful losses covering the rearguard, with a staggering 70 per cent of its strength left dead on the battlefield. As the remnants of the brigade drew near to the German lines, they were in danger of being overtaken by pursuing Red Army units. Wiking's few remaining panzers therefore turned back and held off the enemy for just long enough to allow the last of the brigade to reach the German lines, before being overrun.

Some 32,000 Germans escaped with their lives from the Cherkassy Pocket. Despite the fact that a great deal of equipment had been left behind, a major disaster had been averted. If the pocket had been totally destroyed, Manstein's Army

Left: Time for quick refreshment for this wounded Waffen-SS grenadier. Army commanders often heaped praise on the Waffen-SS in Russia in 1943–44. Wöhler, commander of the Eighth Army, for example, wrote that it 'stood like a rock in the Army, while the enemy broke through in neighbouring sectors.'

Group South would have been dealt a fatal blow.

For the superb performance of their troops, both Gille and SS-Hauptsturmführer Léon Degrelle, commander of *Wallonie*, were taken to Hitler's headquarters in Prussia and decorated. Gille received the Oakleaves and Swords, and Degrelle the Knight's Cross.

The *Das Reich* Division, now totally exhausted, was withdrawn from Russia and sent to France for rest and refitting in February 1944. A battlegroup from the division, under the command of SS-Oberführer Heinz Lammerding, remained on the Eastern Front.

During March 1944, Army Group South was forced to make a slow withdrawal to the River Dniester, on the border with Romania. On 11 March 1944, elements of the *Totenkopf* were airlifted to Balta to form the core of a new defence line.

Above: Waffen-SS troops march past Russian dead in the autumn of 1943. The Leibstandarte *had returned from Italy during this period, and in November, together with two army panzer divisions, had launched a counterattack which retook Zhitomir. By doing so it helped to re-establish the front in that sector.*

Events were moving too fast, however, and both the Sixth and Eighth Armies were too weak to prevent the Red Army from crossing the Dniester on a wide front before the new defences were ready, the Russians pushing deep into Rumanian territory. The *Totenkopf* Division, attached to XLVIII Panzer Corps, battled its way west to avoid encirclement. The exhausted Waffen-SS men fought off the Soviet spearheads for three weeks, as the withdrawal continued through Balta and Rumania, across the River Sireth and into the Carpathians.

The Russian offensive eventually ran out of steam, and the month of May was relatively peaceful. On 9 June, the division was pulled out of the line for rest and refitting, receiving badly needed tanks and other armoured vehicles, as well as around 6000 replacement troops. Some of these men were *Totenkopf* veterans returning to duty after recovering from wounds, but 75 per cent were raw recruits hastily transferred from the newly formed *Reichsführer-SS* Division.

In March 1944, as Army Group South struggled to reorganise its left flank, it was hit by a new Russian offensive which shattered it completely, tearing a massive gap between the 1st and 4th Panzer Armies at Proskurov. Before the breach could be sealed, the entire 1st Panzer Army was surrounded in the Kamenets-Podolsk Pocket. Among the units trapped were the *Leibstandarte* Division and Lammerding's battlegroup.

At this point Hitler agreed to allow the reconstituted II SS Panzer Corps, containing the *Hohenstaufen* and *Frundsberg* Divisions, to be rushed to the Eastern Front. These two divisions, though untried in battle, were of the highest standard. Manned primarily by ethnic Germans, they were equipped and trained to a high level. Also of significance was the fact that the units were built around cadre personnel from tried and tested units, such as *Das Reich* and *Leibstandarte* Divisions, and had been fortunate enough to be allowed 12 months of training. Both units were to display combat performances equal to that of the best Waffen-SS divisions. *Hohenstaufen* was led by SS-Brigadeführer Willi Bittrich and *Frundsberg* by SS-Brigadeführer Karl von Treuenfeld.

As much fuel and ammunition as possible was being airlifted by the Luftwaffe into the Kamenets-Podolsk Pocket in order to avoid

Below: The Waffen-SS in retreat in Russia in 1943. As the Soviet onslaught gathered momentum the Germans experienced a catalogue of defeats: Kharkov was lost, Kiev too, and in October 1943 the Red Army had established a bridgehead on the west bank of the strategically important River Dnieper.

Manstein's forces having to abandon much of their heavy equipment and armour when the time came to break out. On 27 March, under cover of blizzard conditions, the withdrawal began. *Hohenstaufen* and *Frundsberg*, as part of the 4th Panzer Army, took part in the counterattack launched to take the pressure off the retreating 1st Panzer Army as it fought its way west. Contact was made on 7 April, and over the next nine days the bulk of Manstein's forces made it back safely into German-held territory. Unlike the breakout from Cherkassy, this escape was achieved without serious losses. The Soviets, however, lost several hundred armoured vehicles as the Germans headed west.

In April, the *Leibstandarte* was withdrawn from Russia and moved to France for refitting, and Lammerding's battlegroup rejoined the *Das Reich* Division in France. *Hohenstaufen* and *Frundsberg* were withdrawn to Poland, but when the D-Day landings took place in June they were both rushed to France. The *Wiking* Division, badly mauled in the escape from the Cherkassy Pocket, was withdrawn from the front for rest and refitting.

The Waffen-SS in northern Russia

In northern Russia, 1944 had begun badly for the Wehrmacht. The Red Army, having lifted the siege of Leningrad, had gone on to the offensive and gradually drove the Germans westwards towards Estonia and Latvia. It was in this sector of the front that most of the west and east European SS volunteer units were concentrated. The main Waffen-SS force in this area was III (germanisches) SS Panzer Corps, commanded by SS-Gruppenführer Felix Steiner, and containing the 11th SS Freiwilligen Division *Nordland* and SS Freiwilligen Brigade *Nederland*. Within these two units alone were

volunteers from Norway, Denmark, Holland, France, Finland, Sweden and Switzerland. In addition, allocated to the same sector of the front were the 15th and 19th Waffen Grenadier Divisions from Latvia, the 20th Waffen Grenadier Division from Estonia, the Flemish *Langemarck* Brigade and the Sturmbrigade *Wallonie*.

By the end of January 1944, the Red Army had reached the strong German defence lines at Narva. These ran from the city of Narva itself, south along the banks of the River Narva, to the shores of Lake Peipus and down to Polotsk, northwest of Vitebsk. A concentrated effort by the Russians along the entire line was expected. It came on 2 February, but any hopes that the German defences would easily crumble were soon dashed. Narva, the gateway to Estonia, was too important to yield without a mighty struggle. Defensive positions had

Above: During the last two years of the war Waffen-SS divisions were shuttled from one danger spot to another on the Eastern Front in an attempt to avert disaster. The SS units always attacked when committed, which sometimes brought success, sometimes not. But without the Waffen-SS defeat would have come sooner.

therefore been established along the west bank of the River Narva, and for the next few months Steiner's men and other SS units stood firm against overwhelming odds. So prominent were the foreign volunteer units of the Waffen-SS in this sector that the defence of Narva was to become known as the 'Battle of the European SS'.

The Germans had established a large and strongly defended bridgehead covering a substantial area of territory on the eastern approaches to Narva, directly opposite the city itself. At this location soldiers from the *Nordland* Division and Brigade

Nederland dug in and awaited the Russian assault. For the attack on Narva the Red Army had assembled a formidable force: the 8th and 47th Armies and the 2nd Shock Army.

At the beginning of February, the Red Army began its attempts to soften up the German defences with heavy shelling, and some Russian units forced a crossing of the river between Hungerburg and Narva and established a small bridgehead. The Waffen-SS soldiers, however, were able to throw the enemy back with some ease, and on 3 February another attempt by the Russians to establish a bridgehead was defeated by *Nordland*'s 11th Panzer Battalion *Hermann von Salza*. Eventually, the enemy did succeed in establishing a small bridgehead at Ssivertski, to the northwest of the city. A subsequent attempt to break out of the bridgehead into the German rear areas was quickly halted by an SS battlegroup. This Russian pocket among the defenders was finally destroyed in a concerted assault by elements from *Nordland* and *Nederland*.

The bridgehead at Vopsküla

The Soviets forced yet another bridgehead on the west bank at Vopsküla, which was supported by heavy artillery. However, it too was destroyed, by the 19th Waffen-Grenadier Division, after savage hand-to-hand fighting. It was in this action that Estonian volunteer Waffen-Unterscharführer Haralt Nugiseks was decorated for extreme gallantry. His heroism was typical of many SS soldiers who fought at Narva. He had exposed himself to enemy fire on three occasions to urge on his assault troop, on each occasion being hit by enemy fire, yet he continued to lead his men in close-quarter fighting with the enemy, driving them out of their positions. For his actions he was awarded the Knight's Cross on 2

May 1945. Five days later he was captured, and served a long sentence of captivity in a Siberian prison camp.

Frustrated by their lack of success, the Soviets decided to attempt an amphibious assault on the coast to the west of Narva, bypassing the defenders and striking deep into the German rear. This, it was hoped, would lure German units away from the front, thereby weakening the line and creating a chance for a Russian breakthrough.

swiftly crushed, the Russians suffering heavy losses.

To the south, near Krivasso, the Red Army established a strong bridgehead from which to launch its attack into German-held territory. By 24 February, the Soviets looked as though they would break out and sweep up the rear of III (germanisches) SS Panzer Corps. Troops from *Nordland* were quickly moved to the scene and initially made good progress in their counterattack, before becoming bogged down. Then the Soviets counterattacked, and the fighting quickly degenerated into ferocious hand-to-hand combat with knives, bayonets and entrenching tools. Only the arrival of some army Tiger tanks enabled the Waffen-SS troops to withdraw safely. Fierce fighting continued throughout March and April, with the Soviets making little headway against the tenacious German defenders.

Stalemate

When the Waffen-SS troops recaptured Sirgula in March, they discovered the corpses of Estonian civilians who had been used as forced labour to carry ammunition for the Red Army. The Russians had killed the civilians before fleeing. Several Danish SS volunteers had also been captured and shot by the Russians at Hrastovica.

In early March, Soviet artillery and aerial bombardment of the Narva area increased dramatically. On 7 March, for example, massed Russian air attacks went on for 12 hours, to be followed by a massive

The seaborne assault force was ferried in a motley collection of fishing boats and steamers, but did manage to land undetected and overrun the defenders in the immediate area of the beach near Merekula. The defenders were soon alerted,

though, and although the Russian force managed to push forwards into the town, that was as far as it got. German reinforcements were called up in the shape of Waffen-SS grenadiers and Stuka ground-attack aircraft, and the invasion force was

artillery barrage. However, the civilian population of Narva had been evacuated, and the Waffen-SS defenders simply dug deeper into the rubble of the city. The main Russian attack following the softening up was against the area held by the Dutch volunteer *General Seyffardt* Regiment. The Dutch soldiers repulsed every Soviet attack, and even launched their own counterattack. Their commander, SS-Obersturmbannführer Wolfgang Joerchel, was decorated with the

Knight's Cross on 21 April 1944 in recognition of the achievements of his command.

The main axle of the Russian attack then moved against the positions at Lilienbach, held by another Dutch volunteer regiment: *De Ruiter*. After bitter fighting the enemy broke through the Waffen-SS positions, but were driven back by reinforcements from the *Nordland*'s *Danmark* and *Norge* Regiments

Despite the spirited, and often successful, defensive actions by the

Dutch SS troops at Lilienbach, it became clear that this part of the bridgehead on the east bank of the Narva could not be held much longer. Waffen-SS losses in manpower and equipment had been too high, and the Soviet strength was increasing – the Waffen-SS units were being bled white. Nevertheless, by June 1944 the Red Army had still not taken Narva, though the German bridgehead on the east bank, opposite the city, had been drastically reduced. The Germans,

Left: Trapped Waffen-SS men of the Wiking *Division in the Cherkassy Pocket. When Russian forces encircled German units around Korsun and Cherkassy in January 1944, 60,000 troops were trapped. As the Red Army battered the pocket, the* Wiking *and Sturmbrigade* Wallonie *prepared to lead the escape attempt.*

aware of the battering on the central and southern sectors of the front in Russia, realised that their position at Narva was becoming more precarious as each day passed, so it was decided to withdraw to a new defensive position farther west, to the so-called Tannenberg Line.

The final onslaught

On 24 July 1944, the northern end of a massive pincer attack forced the 20th Waffen-Grenadier Division der SS back over the River Narva. The Estonian volunteers were forced to retreat, fighting every metre of the way in defence of their homeland. Having experienced Soviet occupation once before, they had no wish to repeat it, and they fought tenaciously. On 24 July, the Waffen-SS units still on the east bank of the Narva slipped quickly over the river and into the city, destroying the bridges as they did so. By the close of the next day, the city itself had been evacuated. However, during the retreat to the Tannenberg positions the Dutch unit *General Seyffardt* was cut off and annihilated by the Soviets.

On 26 July, the Russian attack against Tannenberg began. The Russians mounted a series of sledgehammer blows against the greatly outnumbered Germans and their European allies. The fighting seesawed back and forth, neither side able to establish a lasting superiority. Despite its many successes, the Waffen-SS suffered great losses, while the enemy poured ever increasing numbers of fresh troops over the Narva and into the battle.

Below: Wiking *troops in the Cherkassy Pocket. As the only armoured formation in the pocket, the* Wiking *Division was tasked with spearheading the breakout. This began on 16 February 1944, and eventually some 32,000 Germans reached safety. However,* Wiking *lost all its vehicles and heavy equipment.*

The Waffen-SS formations had lost virtually all their armour, and their artillery was the only remaining heavy weaponry. The Russian attacks slackened somewhat in August, as the Red Army gathered its strength for one final all-out assault on the beleaguered Waffen-SS. The punch-drunk European volunteers could only await the impending hammer blow.

By this time the European volunteers knew that the Soviet offensive was tearing holes in the front. On 22 June, for example, the Red Army had launched its summer offensive across the entire Eastern Front. Codenamed 'Bagration', it was deliberately timed to start on the third anniversary of the German invasion of Russia. The Red Army had built up a massive force of some six million men, compared to the Wehrmacht's two million. Army Group Centre, which was destined

Right: Reichsführer-SS Heinrich Himmler (with spectacles) inspects Latvian SS soldiers undergoing anti-tank drills near Narva in early 1944. The foreign Waffen-SS recruits who held the Russians at bay at Narva for six months included Danes, Estonians, Dutch, Norwegians and Frenchmen and even some British.

to take the main brunt of the offensive, could field only 750,000 men, under 1000 tanks and 10,000 artillery pieces. Opposing it, however, were over two million Red Army soldiers, 4000 tanks and nearly 29,000 field guns.

Both qualitatively and quantitatively, the Red Army was better. Its conscripts were no longer half-trained, poorly equipped peasants, the types the Germans had faced during the Blitzkrieg in the summer of 1941. By 1944, the Red Army's frontline combat units were composed, in the main, of experienced veterans who had good hardware. The latest T-34 tank, with its uprated 85mm main gun, and the new Josef Stalin heavy tank, armed with a 122mm gun, were a match for most German tanks. In air power, too, the Soviet Air Force was technically equal to the Luftwaffe, having excellent fighters and ground-attack air-

Below: Léon Degrelle, commander of Sturmbrigade Wallonie, marches out of the Cherkassy Pocket. The brigade had put up heroic resistance, but it left the pocket with only 632 men alive. For his bravery and leadership, Degrelle was awarded the Knight's Cross personally by Hitler, while the brigade was withdrawn to regroup.

craft, plus overall superiority in numbers in all theatres.

Although 1943 and the first half of 1944 had been a period of disasters for the armies of the Third Reich on the Eastern Front, Hitler had reason to be greatly pleased with the per-

formance of his elite Waffen-SS divisions. Over and over again SS units had stood firm against almost impossible odds, while Wehrmacht troops retreated. Even the most diehard Waffen-SS troops must have realised that military success on the Eastern Front was now impossible, but they continued to make sacrifice after sacrifice, often holding the line to allow other units to escape.

Few other units in the Wehrmacht could engender such confidence from their Führer as did those of the Waffen-SS. However, though proud of their achievements and their deserved elite status, Hitler's confidence in them was a mixed blessing. With alarming regularity, Waffen-SS divisions were rushed to threatened areas of the front and expected to save the day. That they did so is testament to the fact that they were elite troops. However, they were not invincible, and there would come a time when not even the Waffen-SS could stave off defeat.

Although the Waffen-SS at this point in the war represented only around five per cent of the fighting strength of the Wehrmacht, it is significant that some 20 per cent of the Waffen-SS units were panzer divisions of the highest standard. In fact, just over 25 per cent of all panzer divisions were Waffen-SS, and around 30 per cent of all panzer-

Below: The commander of the Nordland *Division, SS-Brigadeführer Fritz von Scholz, tours the division's defences at Narva. It was part of SS-Gruppenführer Felix Steiner's III SS Panzer Corps. By the end of July most units in the corps had suffered 50 per cent casualties and others had been annihilated.*

grenadier divisions. Yet, despite this fact, apart from the 12 Waffen-SS divisions that could truly be called elite, the remainder were indifferent (see Chapter 9), often, as in the case of those formed late in the war, of divisional strength in name only and sometimes poorly equipped. In view of these figures, the military significance of the Waffen-SS's achievements on the Eastern Front is indisputable.

The tide turns

Despite the Waffen-SS's efforts, the Red Army in the summer of 1944 had only been delayed, not halted. The amount of men and equipment the Russians could put into the field by the middle of 1944 was truly staggering. For the liberation of Byelorussa lone, for example, the Red Army deployed 21 armies, representing a total of 1.4 million men, 31,000 guns and mortars, 5200 tanks

Right: The strain of continuous battle shows clearly on the face of this Waffen-SS soldier. By mid-1944 the Red Army had shattered Army Group Centre, had launched an offensive against Army Group North and was advancing on Army Group North Ukraine. The Germans retreated on all fronts – the end was near.

and assault guns, plus 5000 aircraft. Russian strength was only one part of the equation, though, for Hitler's insistence on no withdrawal aided the Red Army. The Russians simply encircled vast numbers of German units. When Army Group Centre was destroyed some 17 divisions were totally annihilated. The Waffen-SS could only achieve localised successes, and by 1944 even the supermen were faltering. Defeat for the Third Reich was now inevitable on the Eastern Front, the only uncertain factor was when this would occur.

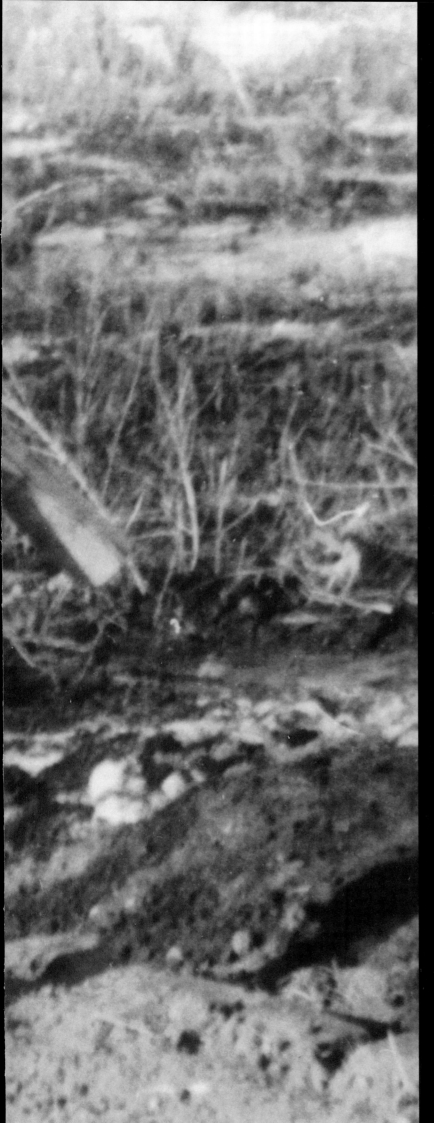

CHAPTER 12

TWILIGHT OF THE GODS

By the end of 1944 it was all too clear that Germany would be defeated. But Hitler still clung to the illusion that victory could be snatched from the jaws of defeat, and once again he looked to his battered Waffen-SS divisions to save his regime. But the supermen failed, and their master turned on them with fury.

Left: The fate of countless thousands of Waffen-SS soldiers on the Eastern Front: a hastily dug grave on foreign soil. By the beginning of 1945, the Third Reich was fighting for survival.

From August 1944, as the Red Army drove through Rumania and Bulgaria, Hitler's east European allies deserted him. As Army Groups E and F, under Field Marshal von Weichs, were forced back through Yugoslavia, the ethnic volunteer SS divisions *Prinz Eugen, Skanderbeg* and *Kama* found themselves not only facing Tito's partisan forces, but also frontline troops of the Red Army. *Skanderbeg* and *Kama* were annihilated, while *Prinz Eugen* was decimated south of Vukovar in January 1945, what was left of it withdrawing into Austria.

In Hungary, the capital Budapest came under the protection of General Otto Wöhler's Army Group South. Units committed to the defence of the city included the 8th SS Kavallerie Division *Florian Geyer*, 22nd SS Freiwilligen-Kavallerie Division *Maria Theresia* and 18th SS Freiwilligen-Panzer-grenadier Division *Horst Wessel*, although some of the latter's units

were sent to Galicia, and others helped suppress the Slovak uprising (August-October 1944).

In October 1944, the Red Army crossed the Hungarian border and raced for the Danube, reaching the river to the south of Budapest and establishing a bridgehead on the west bank, from where it could launch future operations.

To the southwest of the city lay Lake Balaton (the Platensee to the Germans), between which and the area around Budapest the Germans had established strong defensive positions. By 20 December 1944, the Soviets had advanced across the Danube and reached the southern shore of Lake Balaton. The main German defences, however, proved a difficult nut for the Red Army to crack, as by this stage of the war the Germans were making use of natural defence lines, such as rivers, and 'fortress cities'. The Soviets had also overran their supply lines. The breathing space for the Germans

Above: The Waffen-SS in Hungary in December 1944. The attempt to relieve Budapest was a disaster. In Guderian's words: 'I was sceptical since very little had been allowed for its preparation and neither the troops nor the commanders possessed the same drive as in the old days.' This was also true of the Waffen-SS.

was short, though. Marshal Tolbukhin diverted his attack past the eastern edges of Budapest, and with the 6th Guards Tank Army attacking from the northeast and the 46th Army from the south, the city was eventually surrounded in a massive pincer action. Fighting raged for some time, the Soviets unable to rout the Germans and the latter unable to throw back the attackers.

On 26 December, IV SS Panzer Corps, comprising the 3rd SS Panzer Division *Totenkopf* and the 5th SS Panzer Division *Wiking*, were transferred from the Warsaw area in an attempt to relieve Budapest. Two attempts to raise the siege of the city were beaten back by the Soviets, before they in turn launched a counterattack which forced IV SS Panzer Corps on to the defensive. The beleaguered garrison struggled on until 11 February 1945, when some 30,000 of the troops inside the city attempted a breakout to the west. But the retreating Germans were cut to pieces: *Florian Geyer* and *Maria Theresia* were annihilated, and only some 700 troops reached the safety of German lines. Budapest surrendered on 12 February.

The survivors of the two SS cavalry divisions formed the nucleus of a new unit: the 37th SS Freiwilligen-Kavallerie Division *Lützow*, but it never reached the strength of a single regiment, and existed for only three months before being swallowed up in the Russian advance.

The fall of Budapest released a large number of Russian troops for a fresh offensive against the Germans. This threatened the German-held oilfields at Nagykanizsa, Hungary. Hitler was horrified at the thought of losing this precious source of oil, and decided that only a new offensive could throw the Red Army back

over the Danube and save the overall situation in Hungary.

Army Group South, under General Wöhler, comprising the 6th SS Panzer Army, 8th Army, 6th Army and the Hungarian 3rd Army, would strike south from the Margarethe defence lines, while Army Group Southeast's 2nd Army would attack from the west of the Soviet lines. This pincer movement, it was hoped, would crush Tolbukhin's 3rd Ukrainian Front, made up of the 4th Guards Army, 26th Army, 57th Army and 1st Bulgarian Army. IV SS Panzer Corps would remain around Lake Balaton.

The 6th SS Panzer Army

Led by SS-Oberstgruppenführer 'Sepp' Dietrich, the 6th SS Panzer Army consisted of the *Leibstandarte, Das Reich, Hohenstaufen* and *Hitlerjugend* Divisions. The *Leibstandarte*, commanded by SS-Brigadeführer Otto Kumm, and the *Hitlerjugend*, commanded by SS-Oberführer Hugo Kraas, were grouped together as I SS Panzer Corps, while *Das Reich*, temporarily commanded by SS-Standartenführer

Rudolf Lehmann, and *Hohenstaufen*, led by SS-Oberführer Sylvester Stadler, formed II SS Panzer Corps.

The operation was codenamed 'Spring Awakening', but the omens for success were not good. The area around Lake Balaton is predominantly marshy, although under normal circumstances the severe frosts during the early part of the year render the ground hard enough to bear the weight of heavy vehicles. However, in the spring of 1945, the thaw came much earlier than expected and the terrain was turned into a sea of mud, into which 'Sepp' Dietrich's panzers sank, up to their turrets in some extreme instances.

As a preliminary to the main attack, I SS Panzer Corps had smashed the Soviet bridgehead around Estergom with little difficulty. Once the Soviets became aware of a large body of elite Waffen-SS troops in the region, however, they quickly realised that a major offensive was imminent and began to strengthen their defences: increasing the depth of their minefields and preparing anti-tank defences. This

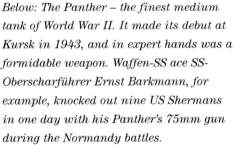

Below: The Panther – the finest medium tank of World War II. It made its debut at Kursk in 1943, and in expert hands was a formidable weapon. Waffen-SS ace SS-Oberscharführer Ernst Barkmann, for example, knocked out nine US Shermans in one day with his Panther's 75mm gun during the Normandy battles.

prelude to the main attack, though successful in its own right, had merely forewarned the Red Army of what was to come.

The day the operation commenced, 6 March, heavy snow had made conditions even worse. I SS Panzer Corps was best placed for the attack, the men having reached their positions in time, but II SS Panzer Corps was still floundering in the mud, its heavy vehicles finding the going almost impossible. Not surprisingly, the German attack began to suffer heavy losses almost from the start. However, the Waffen-SS soldiers threw themselves into the attack with fanatical bravery, driving the enemy back, in the case of I SS Panzer Corps, for distances of up to 40km (25 miles). II SS Panzer Corps however, could only manage penetrations of around 8km (five miles) at best.

The Soviets could make good their losses relatively quickly, while the Germans could only call upon men who were often poorly trained and equipped, and had no motivation to sacrifice their lives at this late stage in the war. The offensive slowed up, and German aircraft began to spot evidence of a massive

Right: A recruiting poster to attract Dutch recruits into the Waffen-SS. Holland supplied SS soldiers until it was overrun by the Western Allies in 1944. The 34th Waffen-Grenadier Division der SS Landstorm Nederland, for example, became operational as a division as late as March 1945, though it was under-strength. It contained members of the Dutch Nazi NSB youth movement, the Dutch equivalent of the Hitler Youth.

Soviet build-up, obviously intended for a counterattack.

The Soviet offensive began on 16 March along the entire sector west of Budapest. The Russian sledgehammer blow stopped the German offensive in its tracks. Dietrich desperately reshuffled his forces to

Left: Waffen-SS troops in retreat after the failure of Operation 'Spring Awakening'. When Hitler learned of this he flew into a rage. He ordered that the soldiers of the Waffen-SS were to remove their cuffbands. When 'Sepp' Dietrich was informed of this, he was astonished and refused to have the order passed on.

reinforce the areas under threat, but when he did so the Soviets soon swamped the areas from which the reinforcements had been taken. The 6th SS Panzer Army was in danger of being cut off, as IV SS Panzer Corps struggled to maintain the German base line. *Das Reich* desperately battled to hold open a corridor of escape for its comrades, but the defection of the Hungarian Army left the flanks of II SS Panzer Corps wide open to the enemy. The Germans had no option but to retreat or lose the best remaining divisions they still possessed on the Eastern Front. By 25 March, the

Russians had torn a 100km (60-mile) gap in the German defences.

As well as the four elite panzer divisions of the 6th SS Panzer Army and the two panzer divisions of IV SS Panzer Corps, the *Reichsführer-SS* Division was also committed to battle around Lake Balaton. The *Horst Wessel* Division had been fortunate enough to escape the encirclement of Budapest and retreat into Slovakia. Within 10 days of the offensive being launched, however, it had been totally wiped out.

Hitler was infuriated at the failure of his Waffen-SS divisions. He demanded the removal of the cuffbands worn by the SS soldiers. Himmler, not having the courage to face his commanders with such an order in person, transmitted it to them in writing instead.

Dietrich, incensed by this insult, ordered his divisional commanders to disobey the order. Despite the wrath of Hitler, the professionalism of the Waffen-SS was such that its units would continue to fight for him and Germany until the end.

After smashing the German offensive around Lake Balaton, the Soviet advance continued to the west of Budapest in a two-pronged movement towards Pápa and Gyór. By 2 April, the Red Army had reached the Neusiedler Lake, on the border between Hungary and Austria, and two days later the last German soldiers had been thrown out of Hungary. The Soviet 46th Army was then transported by boat along the Danube to attack Vienna from the north, while the 4th Guards Army drove towards the city from the

southeast. Of the Waffen-SS divisions which had fought in Hungary, most had withdrawn into Austria to defend Vienna.

Hohenstaufen had been badly mauled in Hungary, so its remnants were formed into small battlegroups, which fought a rearguard action during the withdrawal towards Vienna. The *Totenkopf* also fought in defence of the Austrian capital, while the *Hitlerjugend* withdrew into strong defensive positions

Below: Personnel and vehicles of the 5th SS Panzer Division Wiking *in Austria in early 1945. The division took part in the defensive battles around Warsaw in the autumn of 1944, before being sent south to aid the attempt to relieve Budapest. Withdrawing into Austria, it was decimated in the fighting near Vienna.*

in the mountainous area around Wienerwald, to the southwest of the city, but was forced out of its positions by the unrelenting Soviet pressure after only a few days.

Das Reich put up a stubborn defence to the south of Vienna, before withdrawing into the city itself and becoming involved in bitter fighting around the Florisdorf bridge on 13-14 April. Despite its efforts, it was gradually driven out of the city by intense Russian pressure. Elements continued to fight in the area to the west of Vienna, but the bulk of the division's remnants were sent to the region east of Dresden to help in the futile attempt to hold back Soviet units swarming into Germany itself.

Reichsführer-SS withdrew into Untersteiermark in the south of Austria, but became fragmented. Some units of *Reichsführer-SS* surrendered south of the River Drau, while others withdrew towards Klagenfurt and surrendered to the Americans and British. The *Hitlerjugend* managed to surrender to the Americans at Linz on 8 May. *Hohenstaufen*'s pathetic remnants

surrendered to the Americans at Seyr in Austria, as did the *Leibstandarte*. The *Totenkopf* had withdrawn to the northwest of Vienna and surrendered to the Americans on 9 May. But its members were then handed over to the Russians – few of the Waffen-SS soldiers survived Russian captivity.

The fall of Vienna (13 April 1945) had netted the Soviets over 125,000 prisoners. However, rather than pursue the retreating Germans, Stalin halted major operations in Austria and concentrated on the final push on Berlin.

The northern collapse

In the north, by the spring of 1944, STAVKA had decided that Byeloruss was to be the next major priority for the Red Army. Stalin intended that the Red Army would drive from its starting point, east of Lake Peipus along a line running through Gorki in the centre, skirting the Pripet Marshes, and on to Odessa on the shores of the Black Sea, and push the Germans back some 650km (400 miles) to the very gates of Warsaw. For this it mustered 19 armies and

Above: Waffen-SS tanks in eastern Germany in 1945. The front was collapsing everywhere: on 1 April Army Group B was encircled in the Ruhr and 10 days later the Americans reached the Elbe. On 9 April Königsberg fell to the Russians and Dietrich's SS soldiers had been ejected from Vienna.

two tank armies, with some 1300 or so aircraft in support.

On the night of 22 June 1944, the main assault began, the Russians ripping through Army Group Centre. Within just seven days, the entire length of a 320km (200 mile) front stretching from Ostrov on the Lithuanian border and Kovel on the edge of the Pripet Marshes had been completely overrun. In the weeks that followed, some 350,000 German troops were eliminated.

On 25 June 1944, the *Totenkopf* Division was immediately ordered north from Rumania to help fend off the Soviet attack west of Minsk. The roads, however, were chaotic and the division did not reach its assigned destination until 7 July. By then the Red Army was advancing rapidly towards Grodno, endangering the southern flank of the 4th Army and the northern flank of the battered remnants of the 2nd Army. The *Totenkopf* held the line at Grodno for 11 days against massive odds, before being ordered to withdraw towards the southeast to join the mass of German troops retreating slowly towards Warsaw.

With the Red Army rapidly approaching the Polish capital, the Polish Home Army resistance movement rose up in open revolt against the Germans on 1 August. The Germans were stunned at the initial strength of the uprising, and initially lost almost two-thirds of the city to the valiant Polish fighters. With the Red Army so near, the Poles believed the city would be taken from the Germans.

What the Poles did not realise was that the Red Army's advance was rapidly running out of steam. The Germans were aware of the tired state of the Soviet troops and could concentrate on putting down the uprising (Stalin allowed the Germans to deal with the Poles, as he wanted Poland to be under

Soviet occupation after the war). Just to make sure, he refused the Western Allies the use of Soviet air bases from which to launch supply missions.

To the borders of the Reich

In Warsaw, SS-Obergruppenführer Erich von dem Bach-Zelewski, commander of anti-partisan forces, was determined to crush the Polish revolt with every means at his disposal. The Poles were forced to surrender on 2 October 1944 when their supplies of food and ammunition ran out.

The Soviet offensive had been renewed on 14 August, with an attempt to surround the Polish capital with attacks over the Vistula to the north and west of the city. However, IV SS Panzer Corps, with a powerful force comprising the *Totenkopf* and *Wiking* Divisions, was ready and waiting. For a full week the Russians battered against the German positions without success, and were eventually forced to withdraw to regroup. On 25 August, a massive new offensive was

launched, principally against the *Totenkopf*'s positions, and gradually the Germans were forced to fall back towards Warsaw. The *Totenkopf* Division did attempt a counterattack against the Soviets on 11 September, however, which drove back enemy units. The Soviet steamroller was temporarily halted.

Despite these successes, the *Totenkopf* faced the same problem with regard to being unable to rapidly make good its losses, whereas the Soviets were back up to strength and ready to launch yet another attack against the city by 10 October. This time the weakened Germans were forced back to the northwest of the city, but managed to stabilise their positions quickly and halt the Soviets once again.

By the end of October 1944, Rumania and Bulgaria had capitulated and defected to the Soviets, while in the north Finland had sued for peace terms. The Red Army's 1st Baltic Front had retaken Memel in Lithuania on 10 October, while Yeremenko's 2nd Baltic Front had captured Riga, the Latvian capital.

Below: Armed with an 88mm gun, the Tiger was well armoured and more than a match for the tanks of the Allies, both East and West. Though relatively slow, being fitted with an engine of the same size as that installed in the lighter Panther, in defensive positions it was all but impossible to defeat.

Above: Waffen-SS troops trudge through the rubble of a German town in early 1945. The soldier on the left is armed with an MP43 assault rifle. This 7.92mm weapon had a cyclic rate of fire of 500 rounds per minute and was an excellent piece of hardware. However, like many others, it was too little too late.

The Russian offensives had cut off two entire German armies in Courland, comprising some 33 divisions. Rather than tie up a considerable number of troops in trying to eliminate them, STAVKA chose an air and sea blockade of the pocket.

Among the units able to escape by sea were the remaining Dutch SS volunteers from the *Nederland* Brigade. The ship evacuating them was attacked and sunk, but some of the Dutch SS men did survive and formed the nucleus of the 23rd SS

Freiwilligen Panzergrenadier Division *Nederland*. The unit went back into action at Stargard in Pommerania and also saw action at Stettin, before being forced back towards Berlin.

In January 1945, the Red Army was ordered to drive the Germans out of Poland. Marshal Zhukov and his 1st Byelorussian Front was to drive to Poznan, while Marshal Koniev would direct his assault towards Breslau to the south. Each massive force comprised over one million men, with over 30,000 guns and 7000 tanks between them. Opposing them was a weakened Army Group Centre with 400,000 men and just over 1000 tanks. That said, the Germans still had some 580,000 troops in East Prussia .

On 12 January, Koniev's attack began after a massive artillery bar-

rage lasting 105 minutes. Two days later Zhukov's forces joined in the assault, his forces aiding the Soviet-formed 1st Polish Army in taking Warsaw. During the second half of January the Red Army seized Silesia, one of Germany's most important industrial regions, rich in coal deposits, and by early February had reached the River Oder. Those German strongpoints which had withstood the Soviet onslaught, such as Breslau, were merely bypassed, to be dealt with later.

By the spring of 1945, most of the elite Waffen-SS divisions were carrying out a fighting withdrawal through Hungary and into Austria, while in the central and northern sectors of the Eastern Front those Waffen-SS units still in action were principally east and west European volunteer formations. The level of

determination shown by these volunteers in their attempts to hold the Soviet advance was quite exceptional, if not entirely surprising.

These units raised from eastern European states no longer had any homelands to return to, as their nations had been conquered by the Russians and were now in Stalin's iron grip. The only option was to try and reach the Western Allies to surrender. Those who surrendered to the Soviets, or were handed over to them after giving themselves up to the Western Allies, were usually shot out of hand.

All along the front the Waffen-SS divisions were being destroyed by the Russian onslaught. The *Wiking* Division was decimated in the fighting for the approaches to Vienna. *Nordland* was smashed in the Battle of Berlin; the 14th Waffen-Grenadier Division der SS from the Ukraine surrendered to the Soviets in Czechoslovakia, and the bulk of its surviving personnel were promptly shot. Part of the 15th Waffen-Grenadier Division der SS from Latvia participated in the defence of

Berlin. The *Maria Theresia* Division, predominantly Hungarian, was destroyed in the fighting for Budapest. The Red Army also overran the predominantly Hungarian volunteer 25th and 26th Waffen-Grenadier Divisions while they were still forming. *Nederland*, little more than a regiment, was wiped out in the fall of Berlin, and the battered remnants of the *Langemarck* and *Wallonien* Divisions were also wiped out during the fighting for the Reich's capital city, as were the remaining volunteers of the French *Charlemagne* Division.

Fighting to the end

As the battered German armies on the Eastern Front retreated deep into the Reich, the Waffen-SS divisions were once again to play a major role as rearguard units. *Frundsberg*, serving in Pomerania as part of SS-Obergruppenführer Felix Steiner's 11th Panzer Army in early 1945, took part in an attack on Zhukov's 1st Byelorussian Front as it advanced on Berlin. On 16 February, *Frundsberg*, *Nordland*,

Above: The King Tiger was allocated to Waffen-SS heavy tank battalions. Karl Körner was the commander of one. In April 1945, he encountered Russian tanks: 'I opened fire and destroyed the first and last of the Stalin tanks ... My own personal score of enemy tanks destroyed in this action was 39'.

Nederland and *Wallonien* attacked in a southwesterly direction, smashing into Zhukov's northern flank. The weakened German divisions, however, did not have the strength to seriously deflect the massive Soviet assault and were driven back within a couple of days.

The Russians now took breath for the final push: the capture of Berlin. In the north was Rokossovsky with the 2nd Byelorussian Front, in the centre Zhukov with the 1st Byelorussian Front, and in the south Koniev with the 1st Ukrainian Front. For the Red Army commanders it was to be a race to see who could reach the Reich's capital first. This rivalry was encouraged by Stalin, who used it to get the most out of his commanders.

Zhukov had established a bridgehead over the Oder at Küstrin (which had been taken on 28 March), from where he would launch his attack. Wishing to achieve maximum impact, he decided to open his attack with an artillery barrage of unparalleled ferocity, employing over 8000 artillery pieces in a 30-minute barrage. This would be followed by an immediate and massive assault. Zhukov had nearly 150 searchlights brought up to the launch point, intending to bounce their powerful beams off the low cloud cover and blind the German defenders. Koniev, on the other hand, was taking no

chances, and intended a prolonged barrage of some 145 minutes in length, followed by an attack under the cover of darkness.

The first probing attacks began on 14 April, and, two days later, the main assault began. But the German defenders were aware of Zhukov's plan and withdrew from their positions before the artillery barrage began. Once it had ended they quickly returned to their positions and were waiting for the Soviet assault troops. The searchlight tactic did not work, as they illuminated the attacking Soviets, making them ideal targets. Despite Zhukov's threats, his troops could not throw

the Germans out of their strongly defended positions on the Seelow Heights, opposite his bridgehead. Instead of the immediate victory he had expected, three full days of the most bitter fighting were required before the Germans could be slowly forced back. By 19 April, though, the German defences had been overrun

Below: A British column halts during the drive into the Reich in April 1945. By this time Hitler had lost faith in the Waffen-SS, believing that they had lost heart. In the highly charged atmosphere of the Führer bunker he believed the bizarre. In fact, the Waffen-SS was still fighting to preserve him and his regime.

and the Seelow Heights captured, and Rokossovsky's push from the north launched.

Koniev ordered his 3rd and 4th Guards Tank Armies to break into the city on 20 April, but by the 23rd Stalin had declared that it was to be Zhukov's troops who would make the main assault. Zhukov's men would have the honour of capturing the Führer bunker and the Reichstag itself.

On 21 April, Hitler had ordered an attack to relieve the city. General Theodor Busse, defending the Oder Line with his 9th Army to the south-east of Berlin, was to march to the relief of the city. To the west, General Walther Wenck, holding back the Americans, was to do the same, and Steiner's 11th Panzer Army was to launch an attack from the north to relieve Berlin. But it was all fantasy. If Busse and Wenck

had abandoned their positions to march to the relief of the city, their pitifully few troops would have been instantly overwhelmed. As for Steiner, his 'panzer army' existed on paper only, as his best troops had already been sacrificed or sent into the city: *Nordland* had been sent into Berlin, *Nederland* was sent south to contain a Soviet attack, and the Walloons had been cut to pieces.

By 25 April Berlin was completely surrounded, and the next day 500,000 Red Army troops swarmed into the city itself. The battle for the city was savage, and the Waffen-SS took part in this last battle.

On 28 April, the Soviets broke through the inner city defences and stormed towards the Reichstag. As usual, the SS fought with great courage. The battered building had been turned into a fortress, with heavy machine guns and artillery emplaced behind makeshift gun ports. The first Soviet assault went in on 30 April, supported by artillery and Katyusha rocket launchers. Three battalions of infantry charged forward in the face of heavy fire and managed to breach the defences. Inside the building the fighting

Above: Dead Wiking *personnel in Germany. May 1945. Even in defeat the Waffen-SS displayed an air of superiority. A communique from the* Deutschland *Regiment of 9 May stated: 'completely cut off, without supplies, with losses of 70 per cent. Tomorrow the regiment will march into captivity with heads held high.'*

degenerated into hand-to-hand combat. The SS had turned the cellar into a fortress, and it took two days of heavy fighting before they were defeated. Some 2500 of the Reichstag's defenders were killed, with another 2600 taken prisoner. By that time Hitler was dead and the battle for Berlin was over. At 1500 hours on 2 May, Lieutenant-General Weidling surrendered the city to the Russians. There were still groups of Waffen-SS troops fighting in various pockets of the shrinking Reich. They continued to fight until all the formal surrender negotiations had been completed. The Waffen-SS had, like the Wehrmacht, failed to bring the Führer victory, but it had fought with courage and tenacity throughout. But there was another side to its actions: the atrocities committed by Hitler's elite.

CHAPTER 13

ATROCITIES AND WAR CRIMES

The Waffen-SS was the spearhead of Nazi aggression. Ruthless in battle, disparaging of the notion of the worth of human life, even their own, Waffen-SS soldiers were quite capable of committing atrocities on and off the battlefield. This was particularly true in the East, where the Waffen-SS faced the 'true' enemies of Nazism: the Jews, Bolsheviks and 'subhumanity' in general.

Left: Waffen-SS soldier shooting 'undesirables' in Russia. The Leibstandarte *was one SS unit which was indicted at Nuremberg for committing atrocities against civilians in Russia.*

The soldiers of the SS were the standard bearers of National Socialism. They could be hard, ruthless and capable of savage behaviour. The regime they served taught that some races, notably the Slavs, were subhuman, whereas the SS was a racial and biological elite. The de-humanisation of certain groups – Jews, Slavs, communists – resulted in the shooting of prisoners, the murder of civilians and indiscriminate destruction. This chapter will examine some notable examples of the consequences of ideologically indoctrinated soldiers.

Nazi atrocities in Poland

After the victory in Poland, the Führer's social plan for the country was simple. The first phase was the murder of the country's cultural and political elite, but Hitler realised this was no undertaking for regular soldiers. Himmler was ordered to form units that were innocuously named Einsatzgruppen, or Task Forces, to follow the German troops and liquidate as they went. Himmler entrusted this mission of mass killing to mobile Sicherheitsdienst SD and Sipo Security Police detachments. In preparation for the planned expansion east, SS-Obergruppenführer Heydrich commissioned Walter Schellenberg, one of his most brilliant protégés, to work out a plan for fusing the state organisation, the Sicherheitspolizei (Sipo), the security police on which the Gestapo depended, with the party organisation, the Sicherheitsdienst (SD), thus creating an organisation which would oversee the Einsatzgruppen in Poland. The organisation known as the Reichssicherheitshauptamt, (RSHA) or Reich Main Security Office, came into being in September 1939. Its formation was based on a compromise, according to which certain of its sections were placed under state authority and others under that of the Nazi Party.

For the Polish campaign, six Einsatzgruppen of 400 to 600 men were formed. One was assigned to each of the five invading armies, while a sixth unit was deployed in the border province of Poznan, a former Prussian territory that Hitler intended to reclaim for the Reich. As the German Army raced across Poland the SS followed, performing with vigour its own part in the destruction of that nation. Behind the advancing armies hastily improvised reception camps were constructed. The Einsatzgruppen worked methodically from previously prepared lists of names. Government officials, local political leaders, aristocrats, priests, business people, teachers and physicians were prime targets for murder, as were the Jews. All who could be found were rounded up and herded into these camps, where execution by shooting usually took place soon afterwards. A German diplomat described it in his diary: 'the SS reign of terror in Poland progressed efficiently.' Seven days after the invasion,a death toll of 200 Poles a day was claimed by SS commanders, and 20 days later Heydrich stated: 'of the Polish upper classes in the occupied territories only a maximum of three per cent is still present.'

Death squads

Soon death squads of another variety, the so-called Home Defence units, began operating alongside members of the Einsatzgruppen. They consisted of ethnic Germans who had been objects of German-Polish rivalry since the inception of the Polish Republic in 1918. German-Polish relations had deteriorated steadily, especially in the always tense areas of relations between the Poles and the Nazi-dominated government of the Free City of Danzig in East Prussia. The Home Defence units were driven by a lust for revenge. As soon as the Wehrmacht

had rolled past, men from the German minority banded together in Volunteer Militias that soon degenerated into marauding bands bent upon killing Poles. In Western Prussia, anti-Polish feeling was rife and here Albert Forster, the Gauleiter of Danzig, did everything he could to fan the flames of hatred.

Himmler saw in Forster an old adversary who was gathering influence, and he was not pleased by this encroachment onto his preserve.

Himmler, who always protected what he regarded as his domain, dispatched Gottlob Berger, the Chief of the Recruiting Office, to take charge and bring the Home Defence units under SS control. They were divided into four groups and each assigned a German SS commander. Although they were to serve as auxiliary police forces, some units continued on their murderous endeavours, causing even Heydrich to show concern. However, the lack of discipline

worried him more than the lack of humanity shown by these newly recruited SS men.

As the SS-Verfügungstruppe receive its baptism of fire, the SS-Totenkopfverbände received its initiation in blood, being employed in terrorising the civilian population through acts that included hunting down straggling Polish soldiers and torturing and murdering large numbers of Poland's population. Their military capacities were directed to

Above: An example of the SS reign of terror in Poland. Though it was the Einsatzgruppen which were largely responsible for the rounding up of Jews and members of the Polish intelligentsia, they were assisted by the Waffen-SS. Totenkopf units were actively involved, killing and torturing randomly.

the task of confiscating agricultural products and livestock.

On 7 September Himmler, with the purpose of achieving Hitler's aims of destroying all Polish resistance and leadership, deployed three Totenkopf regiments – *Oberbaynern*, *Brandenburg*, and *Thüringen* – as independent SS-Einsatzgruppen under Eicke's overall command. Eicke had bestowed upon him the lofty official title of Höhere SS und Polizei Führer (Higher SS and Police Leader) for the regions of Poland conquered by 7th and 10th Armies. He was assigned to Hitler's special headquarters train and did not accompany the SS-Totenkopfverbände into the field.

The three Death's Head regiments and the units of the security police and SD were released from direct army control and acted as the supreme police authority of the Reich in the provinces of Poznan, Lodz and Warsaw under Eicke's direction. The Death's Head regiments continued in this rôle until early October, when they were withdrawn to be reorganised into the cadre of the *Totenkopf* Division.

A trusted Eicke subordinate, Standartenführer Paul Nostitz, commanded the SS-Totenkopf Standarte *Brandenburg*, and carried out his orders thoroughly and fanatically. On 13 September 1939, SS-*Brandenburg* moved into Poland to begin 'cleansing and security measures'. It secured villages from 'insurgents,' conducted house searches and arrested large numbers of 'suspicious elements.' Nostitz described in his report how insurgents, plunderers, Poles, and Jews were liquidated in large numbers; many of them were shot 'while trying to escape.'

Atrocity at Leslau and Bomberg

The people of Leslau (Wloclanek) and Bomberg (Bydgoszcz) were to experience the savage measures *Brandenburg* meted out. The first was Leslau, which lies some 112km (70 miles) northwest of Warsaw on the Vistula on 22 September. Thus began a four-day Judenaktion, or Jewish action. The city's synagogues were subjected to dynamiting and burning while the Jewish shops were plundered. Many leading members of the local Jewish community were arrested and executed. SS-Gruppenführer Günther Pancke visited Nostitz in the midst of the Leslau action, and delivered a top secret order from Eicke to Nostitz instructing him to dispatch two battalions of *Brandenburg* to Bomberg (Bydgoszcz) to conduct an 'intelligentsia action' there. This was done on 24 September, and during the following two days the SS troops hunted down 800 Polish civilians ear-

Left: Fritz Knöchlein of the Totenkopf *Division, who was responsible for the Le Paradis massacre in May 1940. After having the British prisoners machine-gunned, he then ordered his men to bayonet and shoot in the head any who still showed signs of life. He was hanged by the British in 1949.*

Right: Wilhelm Mohnke of the Leibstandarte *Division. In May 1940, he had British prisoners murdered at Wormhoudt by herding them into a barn and then having grenades thrown in. This was followed by small-arms fire. Those who survived were then dragged outside and shot dead.*

marked as potential trouble makers and shot them.

Other atrocities were committed in the German 10th Army's rear area, in the province of Kielce in south-central Poland. In Nisko, Rawa, Mazowiecka and Ciepielow, incidents occurred involving the torture and execution of large numbers of Jews, political and religious leaders and captured Polish soldiers. The other two SS-Totenkopfverbände, *Oberbayern* and *Thüringen*, operated behind Reichenau's 10th Army and received orders to conduct actions against Polish Jews and civilians similar to the measures taken by *SS-Brandenburg*. These mass shootings were almost certainly the work of these two Death's Head regiments which were under the Eicke's command.

Condemnation from the army

The baptism of fire the Verfügungstruppe so desperately desired was obtained in the war against Poland, their troops having suffered proportionally much heavier casualties than the army. However, there was no commendation from the Army High Command for the contribution the SS played in the campaign. On the contrary, the generals of the OKH expressed only negative views and were quick to point out that the disproportionate casualty figures were attributable because the SS had not been properly trained for the job, particularly its officer corps. As for the SS-Totenkopfverbände, it engendered an attitude of uneasiness, tempered with shock and disgust among responsible senior offi-

cers of the German Army. The real purpose behind the presence of the Totenkopfverbände in Poland was perceived by the shrewder army commanders. Army sentiment and suspicion was put on record by General Boehm-Tettelbach in his report to the 8th Army, in which he was of the clear impression that SS-*Brandenburg* had been sent to Leslau with the prime objective of taking violent action against the Jews. Nostiz's repeated refusal to

perform normal security duties, such as combing the forests south of Leslau with the SS-*Brandenburg*, was cited to support his claims. The general also highlighted how SS-Gruppenführer Pancke had said openly that the SS had special tasks to perform that were outside the competence of the army, and therefore the SS-Totenkopfverbände would not obey army orders. In fact, the torment of Jews and other Polish civilians was preferred by the

SS officers and men who remained in Leslau. The reports undoubtedly reached Colonel-General Blasko-witz, who found the Death's Head units loathsome. The atrocities committed in Leslau by SS-*Brandenburg* helped transform him into the army's most bitter critic of SS behaviour in Poland. In a protest to Colonel-General Walther von Brauchitsch, the Commander-in-Chief of the German Army, he composed a long memorandum cataloguing the crimes committed by the SS-Totenkopfverbände in Poland and sent it to him.

The Einsatzgruppen

The activities of the Einsatzgruppen had begun to be questioned by many German soldiers. Their heinous enterprises were to be camouflaged by such euphemisms as 'counter-espionage work' in the attempt to keep them secret from the regular forces. The 14th Army's operational section reported on 20 September that the 'troops are especially incensed that instead of fighting at the front, young men should be demonstrating their courage against defenceless civilians.' In the Operational Zone the Einsatz-gruppen were technically under army command, and more than one senior Wehrmacht officer was becoming worried at the consequences. Admiral Wilhelm Canaris, the Chief of the Abwehr, or military intelligence, informed the High Command that 'the world will one day hold the Wehrmacht responsible for these methods since these things are taking place under its nose.'

Before the Polish campaign, Hitler had given the German military notice that activities would be conducted in the conquered region that they might find unsavoury. Their ability to react is illustrated in the case of a member of the SS artillery regiment and an army military policeman, who, during the height

of the campaign, shot 50 Jews who had been conscripted for forced labour. The local army commander demanded they be tried by court-martial, and although the prosecuting officer called for the death penalty, the murderers were sentenced to short prison terms for manslaughter.

In the 'New Europe' which Hitler intended to create, there would be no place for Poland, even its name was to disappear. After the defeat of that country in October 1939, large areas of northern Poland were

Above: Waffen-SS soldiers in Russia. Himmler stressed the nature of the war in Russia to his commanders: 'I ask you to look after them [their men], and guide them, and not let them go before they are really saturated with our spirit ... We have only one task – to stand firm and carry on this racial struggle without mercy.'

incorporated into the Reich as Gau Danzig-West Prussia and Gau Possen, which was later to be renamed Gau Wartheland after the River Warthe which flows through it. The rest of pre-war Poland was

of feudal peasant aristocracy which had always been one of his dearest fantasies. To make room for them, the indigenous Slavs and Jews would be removed or reduced to serfdom. The SS readily played its part in this grand scheme.

On the battlefield the soldiers of the Waffen-SS could be just as brutal. Taught to hold their own lives in low esteem, it was easy for them to commit atrocities against prisoners. On 27 May 1940, for example, during the campaign in the West, near the village of Le Paradis, 100 men of the British 2nd Royal Norfolk Regiment had held up the *Totenkopf* Division. SS-Obersturmbannführer Fritz Knöchlein, who commanded the 3rd Company, 2nd SS-Totenkopf Regiment, was pinned down for nearly an hour by rifle and machine-gun fire which killed and wounded several of his men.

Massacre at Le Paradis

The defenders ran out of ammunition and decided to surrender. Knöchlein had them searched, then marched them across the road into a barnyard, placed against a wall and had them shot. The gunners continued until all cries were extinguished. Knöchlein then detailed a squad to bayonet and shoot in the head any who still showed signs of life (Privates Albert Pooley and William O'Callaghan survived). Knöchlein was subsequently tried by a British court, found guilty and sentenced to death. He was hanged in 1949 in Hameln, Weser, a British controlled penitentiary.

Another atrocity took place later during the campaign at Wormhoudt after the *Leibstandarte* had taken some British prisoners. One group of between 80-90 Royal Warwicks, Cheshires and a few artillery men were observed by the commander of the 2nd Battalion, SS-Oberführer Wilhelm Mohnke, one of the original members of the *Leibstandarte*, late

renamed 'The General Government' and placed under the control of Governor General Hans Frank. In October Himmler, to further his dream of a racially pure Greater Germany, had embarked on another venture and become czar of a cruelly ambitious scheme for the resettlement of Poland. This was to affect the lives of more than a million Eastern Europeans and prompted a high-ranking SS racial specialist to enthuse, 'The East belongs to the SS.' As with many of Himmler's projects, resettlement began with less

grandiose proportions. The advance of the Soviet Army into Eastern Poland during September had resulted in some 136,000 ethnic Germans being placed under Soviet domination. This situation was unacceptable to Berlin and the SS. In discussions with the Soviets it was agreed to let these people leave and, in addition, it was negotiated for the transfer of another 120,000 Germans living in the Baltic states. Newly conquered Poland would be the ideal place to resettle the ethnic Germans, perhaps even in the kind

in the afternoon. He lost his temper and accused the NCO in charge of the escort of disobeying orders by taking prisoners instead of killing them. Mohnke ordered them to be escorted to a nearby barn and disposed of. A salvo of grenades was first thrown into the small, crowded barn. This was followed by small-arms fire. The survivors were ordered out in groups of five. The first two groups to appear were immediately executed, one private, although badly wounded, feigned death and later managed to crawl into the barn and lie among the dead. Fifteen survived the massacre, although one was to die shortly afterwards. When four of the survivors were repatriated in 1943, they made the British authorities aware of the incident. Terrible though this action was, it paled beside Waffen-SS atrocities committed in Russia, during the 'holy crusade' in the East against Bolshevism and Jewry

SS-Oberführer Max Simon, commander of the SS-Totenkopf Infanterie Regiment 1, exhorted his troops to be even more brutal than before, declaring that the Russians were 'bandits who must be slaugh-tered without pity.' It is said that partisans captured by *Totenkopf* troops were often executed by shots to the stomach to ensure a slower, more agonising death. Whether this is true or not, it certainly illustrates the sinister reputation these men were rapidly earning. The skills these hardened *Totenkopf* troops had learned in Eicke's concentration camps were much in demand in Russia. At one stage, an entire battalion from Einsatzgruppe A was transferred to the division as battle casualty replacements. It is also interesting to note that of the main atrocities which were committed by Waffen-SS troops during World War II, almost all were by units under the command of officers who had previously served in Eicke's *Totenkopf* Division. For soldiers imbued with the ideology of National Socialism,

Right: The reality of SS rule in Russia: wanton killing. In Minsk, for example, as one Wehrmacht observer wrote: 'The SD one day took about 280 civilian prisoners from the jail, led them to a ditch and shot them. Since the capacity of the ditch was not exhausted, other prisoners were pulled out and also shot.'

and hardened by the leadership of Theodor Eicke, it was impossible to show mercy towards the foe.

Despite the more positive reputation the division was to earn for its tenacity in battle, and the gallantry of many of its individual soldiers, it was ultimately to be fatally compromised by the regular interchange of its men with those from the concentration camps. *Totenkopf* soldiers who were no longer able to serve at the front through illness or injury often found themselves posted to the camps, and many of the younger camp personnel on reaching the age of conscription found themselves in the *Totenkopf* Division.

By the summer of 1941, when the *Leibstandarte* stood poised on the eastern borders of the Reich, ready to strike into Russia as a part of Hitler's invasion force assembled for Operation 'Barbarossa', it had

gained a fine reputation for gallantry and elan, and, apart from the incident at Wormhoudt, could be justifiably proud of its achievements.

War in the East, however, introduced the young Waffen-SS grenadiers to a far more brutal and unrelentingly savage form of warfare. The SS had been taught to regard the Russians as despised and hated communist enemies. The Soviets, for their part, saw the Germans as hated fascist invaders. This mutual aversion expressed itself on the field of battle in fierce hand-to-hand fighting, with no quarter being asked or given. What may be acceptable in the heat of battle, however, is an entirely different matter outside combat, and the *Leibstandarte* was accused of the cold-blooded murder of a large number of Soviet prisoners of war in October 1941 during the battle for Taganrog. The *Leibstandarte*'s commander, 'Sepp' Dietrich, did give an order that for a period of several days no enemy prisoners were to be taken, in reprisal for Soviet atrocities against his own men.

The war on the Eastern Front was a particularly savage and ruthless affair. The Soviets were fighting for their very existence, and even some of their own people were volunteering to fight for the Germans against them. No mercy was shown to the hated invaders.

In the West, in general, the conduct of warfare rarely degenerated to the level of savagery common in the East, and in general the rules of

Left: One of the worst Waffen-SS units for committing atrocities. Members of the Dirlewanger *Brigade photographed during the Warsaw uprising. Commanded by Oskar Dirlewanger and composed of criminals, cashiered officers and SS soldiers on punishment, it killed, raped and looted its way through Warsaw.*

Sturmbannführer Diekmann was dispatched with a company of troops to investigate.

On his arrival at Oradour he sealed the village, rounded up all the inhabitants and exacted his revenge. In the violence that followed, 642 people of all ages and sexes, including 207 children, were either shot or herded into buildings and burned to death. When Diekmann reported back to his unit, his commander was furious at his conduct and immediately called on the divisional commander, SS-Brigadeführer Lammerding, to institute court martial proceedings. However, Diekmann was killed in action shortly afterwards.

The Malmédy massacre

The other major incident which occurred during the Western Campaign in 1944 was the massacre of a number of American POWs at Malmédy. There is no real controversy over what happened. A number of American prisoners had been assembled at the Baugnez crossroads, near Malmédy, as spearhead units of I SS Panzer Corps streamed past. They were guarded by two Mk IV tanks and their crews. German sources claim that only some 20 POWs were involved, Belgian witnesses say around 35, and the Americans claim over 120. Whatever the numbers involved, a Rumanian *Volksdeutsche* named Georg Fleps, fired his pistol into the mass of prisoners. As they scattered the other Germans opened fire and most of the prisoners were killed.

The Warsaw uprising in 1944 was another venue for a Waffen-SS

atrocity, this time involving two of the most notorious military formations in history: the 29th Waffen-Grenadier Division der SS (russische Nr 1) and the 36th Waffen-Grenadier Division der SS.

Both units, though nominally of divisional status, were in fact only of brigade strength. The 29th Waffen-Grenadier Division was commanded by Bronislav Kaminski and consisted of anti-communist Russians who had previously been engaged in suppressing Soviet partisan activity. The 36th Waffen-Grenadier Division was recruited from the lowest criminal elements who could be dredged from the prisons and concentration camps of the Third Reich.

The Warsaw uprising

Under the command of SS-Oberführer Oskar Dirlewanger, who had himself been imprisoned by the Nazis for a string of crimes, including sexual offences against a young girl, this unit and Kaminski's men had no compunction in conducting themselves with the utmost barbarity. The catalogue of atrocities committed by these men revolted those German frontline combat troops involved in the fighting for Warsaw, and complaints from senior German military officers flooded in. The troops of both Waffen divisions even threatened any German Army troops who tried to interfere with their debauchery, as they indulged themselves in an orgy of looting, rape, torture and murder.

Eventually Himmler was forced to act. Kaminski was now too much of an embarrassment to the SS and was murdered, his death being explained to his men as the result of an attack by Soviet partisans. Dirlewanger survived the war, but was beaten to death by former concentration camp inmates.

This then was the dark side of the Waffen-SS. In the final analysis, the Black Guard had a black heart.

warfare were more or less adhered to. There were, nevertheless, some incidents which did serve to blacken the reputation of Waffen-SS.

In the summer of 1944 in France, as the *Das Reich* Division prepared to head northwards to the Normandy battlefields, it was tasked with the suppression of partisan activity in the region around Limoges. Following the death of one of the division's officers, the village he identified of Oradour-sur-Glane was implicated. Because of this, SS-